Legends of the Lakota

The Indian Historian Press
San Francisco

Legends of the Lakota

James LaPointe

Illustrated by Louis Amiotte

The Indian Historian Press
American Indian Educational Publishers
San Francisco

Contents

Land Ceded by the Sioux since 1868

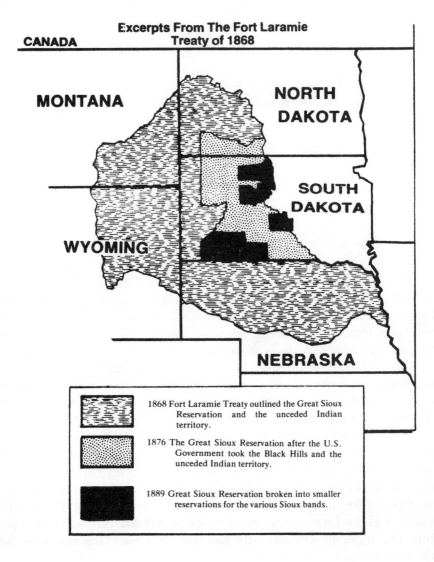

Excerpts From The Fort Laramie Treaty of 1868

CANADA

MONTANA

NORTH DAKOTA

SOUTH DAKOTA

WYOMING

NEBRASKA

1868 Fort Laramie Treaty outlined the Great Sioux Reservation and the unceded Indian territory.

1876 The Great Sioux Reservation after the U.S. Government took the Black Hills and the unceded Indian territory.

1889 Great Sioux Reservation broken into smaller reservations for the various Sioux bands.

Preface

IT WAS LATE IN LIFE that I decided to write these Lakota legends, as the old-time storytellers used to tell them. Why late in life? I suppose the reasons can be traced to my own inadequacies. Indecisions, misgivings of the white man's attitudes, real and imagined, restrained me. I could not imagine a white publisher showing interest in Indian legends, particularly if written by an Indian.

In my senior year in school I was fortunate in having my story accepted for the annual yearbook. The English teacher, a thin, austere person, took me aside and confided that my story had been selected only on its uniqueness, and that I mustn't harbor any notions of future writing, as my work showed no particular merit and had no literary value and certainly no promise of talent. Perhaps that also had a restraining effect on me, because I believed the old girl. She could parse eloquently; she knew syntax, rhetoric, semantics. She could analyze the beat of every poem ever written, I do believe. I guess I never had much faith in myself. Anyway, I simply wrote the legends without any thought of presenting them to the public view.

My own children enjoyed them, however. I loved telling these ancient tales, and watching the wide-eyed, wondering faces of the little ones.

In these legends I use some Lakota words. They are

spelled phonetically, so that they can be pronounced with some degree of similarity to the language. The word "Sioux" is one originating with the French, and derives from the Chippewa word *Naduwessi*, meaning enemies or snakes, according to most accounts. The word was later shortened to Sioux. The Sioux are known as *Dakota* speakers. The Sioux Nation may be divided into three groups. The "D" people lived in the eastern part of the domain. The "L" people occupied the middle and southern portions, and the "N" people owned the northwest regions. Thus, our alphabets and the English-Lakota dictionaries differ; the pronunciations and meanings of many words have wide variations. The Teton Dakota speak the so-called "L" dialect. Their bands are: Oglala (those who scatter); Sichanhgu (burned twigs, called Brule by the French); Minneconjou (those who plant by the water), Sans Arc (the French expression for "without bows"); Two Kettles, Blackfeet and Hunkpapa.

As a guide, I will give only the vowel sounds, since they are constant) A as in *far*; E as *wet*; I as in *wit*; O as in *boat*; and U as in *tulip*. I'm no academic or linguistic authority on the Sioux language, and I'm open to contradiction. It is the language of my childhood, my first tongue, and I feel free and comfortable in it.

I am indebted to Bea Medicine, a distinguished Sioux scholar, for this explanation of the tribes belonging to the Siouan language stock:

The Plains Tribes: Assiniboine (*N*akota);
        Crow
     Dakota
       Teton (*L*akota)
       Yankton (*D*akota)
       Sisseton

The Village Tribes: Hidatsa, Mandan, Ponca, Omaha, Iowa, Missouri, Oto, Kansa, Osage. The Catawba were an eastern group of Siouan speakers.

In the record books it is recorded I was born April 6, 1893, on the Pine Ridge Reservation, somewhere near the place now known as the Wounded Knee Battlefield.

Like any young child, my earliest recollection of life was one of wonder. Croaking frogs, toads exuding a slimy fluid when picked up, a mother-fish herding a myriad of little ones. These simple things I found fascinating. Nothing was bad. People were all good. There was a sense of constant movement, or so it seemed. People were usually moving about in groups. I remember log cabins mixed together with tipis. And then, noisy children at play, the singing of the older ones, the barking of dogs; all these are remembered sounds. Many horses scattered over the grassy hills, campfires flickering at early dusk down the valley, tipis dimly lighted casting huge shadows on the walls. These were the scenes etched upon my mind. Inside the tipis the elders talked, the little ones listened. Only one voice was heard at a time. That was the courtesy accorded each to the other. I was conscious of my very being, and keenly aware of my surroundings. It was a good many years later that the realization dawned on me that I was an Indian, as differentiated from the white man.

Although there are many legends based in other parts of the Lakota world, and in other aspects of Lakota life and belief, the Paha Sapa (Black Hills) seemed to be the focal point for the legends most vividly remembered . . . held in my mind, so to speak. These legends, therefore, are about the Black Hills of South Dakota.

White men have built altars upon which they communed with their God. Taku Wakan, God of the redman, created a special altar, the Paha Sapa (so they say), upon which the Western Indian, for ages, had made desperate efforts to reach his God. I say "desperate efforts" because in some of the rituals there is an element of self-torture. But then, of course, so too do some religious orders of the white man inflict torture on themselves, for example by wearing hair shirts, practicing self-denial and in other ways attempting to reach their God.

The birth of many a legend was founded upon the eulogizing of some particular spot in the Black Hills. These legends, the factual events related in story form, and the practice of religious rituals, as I have heard them in my youth, will remain with me forever, although they are becoming hazy now, and seem almost a dream.

My father, a kind and tender man, died when I was four years old. What hurts I may have suffered, I was too young to evaluate or even to grasp their full impact. My young life was serene enough until I was ten, when I first had a sizable taste of the woes of life.

Early in August, 1903, while the menfolk were all busy putting up hay, a white man in a livery rig came to us. He talked at some length with my uncle. After he went away the uncle told me that a brother and I were signed up to attend school, far away in some city. I wasn't worried. In fact I was rather elated, visualizing new wonders to explore and marvel at.

All too soon it was time to go. After the hurried hair cuts and the hasty washing up, we were taken to the railroad town like sheep to slaughter. An odor of burning coal permeated the air and the stores had some kind of a fruity smell. Togged up in new store-bought

3

clothes, we proudly strutted, unmindful of the next day.

Early the next morning we were herded to the depot. A train with a glaring headlight soon came puffing in. Dazedly we boarded the steel monster. The coach we entered was full of smoke and strange, be-whiskered men; some were sleeping. The mournful whistle of the engine and the endless clacking of the rails as the train sped along, were sounds that remained with me for many days.

It was ages, it seemed, when at last the train made its stop in Rapid City, South Dakota. A kindly conductor, who may have understood our predicament, gently helped us off the train and turned us over to a tall man. He in turn herded us into a long lumber wagon and there was another jolting ride of two miles, until we finally arrived at our future home. The many children already there gave us the silent once-over. We must have been a sorry sight; some of us were weeping.

There were further worries. I was separated from my brother and taken to another part of the big house, where there was a collection of woe-begone little boys.

A stern-faced woman had charge of us. At noontime, in military style, we marched into the dining hall and were seated, ten at each table. A prayer was dutifully mumbled, and then a bell clanged. Like magic, the meat and bread disappeared from the table, leaving only gravy and potatoes. Darwin's theory of evolution— survival of the fittest—was neatly demonstrated. I didn't care. I couldn't have swallowed anything. A big lump was pushing up in my throat.

In the evening, again in military fashion, we marched to the assembly hall. The formidable scowling man was the same huge person I had seen back on the reservation prairies. I think he gave us a pep talk. I didn't understand nor even hear a thing. The reception being ended, we marched out, keeping step to the pounding of a piano. Suddenly that big man slapped me on the back of the head, knocking me against the boy ahead of me. "Get in step there," he commanded. A lonely, terrified Indian boy keeping step? Right there, he made a rebel out of me. He didn't even give me time to shed my coma of despair.

Along with our ever-present loneliness we had to deal with our empty stomachs. We stole potatoes, carrots, turnips and corn from the fields. We parched the corn, baked the potatoes in ashes and ate the carrots and turnips raw. We fished a lot and lived on boiled suckers and sold our trout to white fishermen for nickels and dimes, depending on their size. For a nickel we could buy a hat full of apples from the orchard. We borrowed the biggest hats whenever we

4

went shopping for apples. We survived.

After World War I, I returned to the reservation to take my place in the flow of life and to begin assuming a few responsibilities. It wasn't easy. I found that all the oldtime storytellers had now joined the silent marchers upon that mysterious trail, the Milky Way, their faces toward *Wanaghiyata*, (Spirit World).

Even my grandmother, a slight, energetic woman with an acute mind and a flawless memory, had passed on. This grandma was quite a lady. Like a she-bear, she was fiercely possessive and protective. We little ones felt safe whenever she was around. She told us she was gifted with energy and a bright mind because a mystic thing had happened the year of her birth. The "Snowstorm of the Stars," as the Lakota say, occurred, a celestial display of countless stars appeared, seeming to change positions in the sky. It was the year of the heavenly meteoric spectacle of 1833.

It was tragic to me, that those storytellers, always welcome in any tipi, were dying away, taking their wealth of legendry and information with them. I tried to make others see this great loss. No one had the time. Life had become complex and highly competitive; it was a constant struggle to provide for a decent living. I didn't blame anyone. "Bringing home the tallow" had become more important.

Most of the oldtime storytellers are gone now, home to a better place, I hope. Only a few of us remain who remember those tales and legends, and the lively, sometimes dramatic way they were told. I was a starry-eyed, delighted child when I heard them first. I would like to dedicate these ancient oft-told tales now to the whole world of starry-eyed children, both young and old, hoping they will find the same delight and wonder in them that I did so very long ago.

The reader should be aware of the fact that the legends and stories that follow are not precisely the ancient, traditional, religious or ritual legends told by the elders before white contact. By the time I heard them, a good deal of those old legends had been adapted through influences of another civilization, another set of religious beliefs, creating a blend of the old and the new. However, they were and are still today just as enchanting and descriptive of many ancient beliefs, as when I heard them first.

James LaPointe

The Pine Ridge Indian Reservation
The Districts

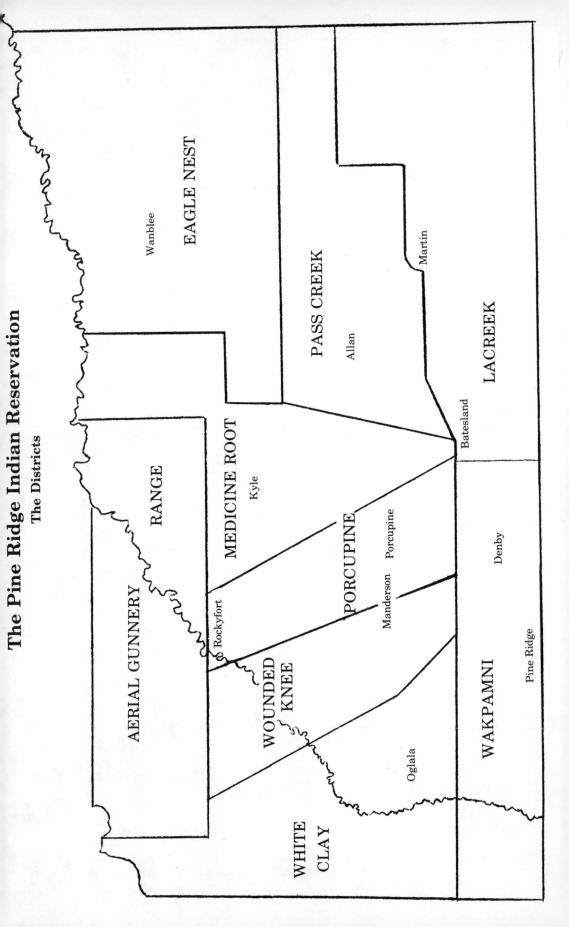

EAGLE NEST

Wanblee

PASS CREEK

Martin

Allan

LACREEK

Batesland

AERIAL GUNNERY

RANGE

MEDICINE ROOT

Kyle

PORCUPINE

Porcupine

Manderson

Denby

Rockyfort

WOUNDED KNEE

WAKPAMNI

Pine Ridge

Oglala

WHITE CLAY

Introduction

EARLY IN THEIR ANCIENT HISTORY, the Lakota received the most important symbol of their religion, the Sacred Pipe. (The Cross, as one example, may be compared to the Sacred Pipe in religious importance.) So strongly have the people believed in it, that its use has remained constant even into modern times.

The Pipe is symbolic of the universe. Its bowl is made of red stone signifying mother earth. The wooden stem represents all growing things. The eagle feathers hanging from the Pipe symbolize the heavens and all things that fly. The center of the bowl represents the universe itself. In every ceremony, the Pipe is always filled in the same ritual manner.

A pinch of tobacco is offered to the four cardinal directions, to the earth and the sky. Only then is the tobacco placed in the Pipe. A small cherry stick, made from the peeled ark of the red willow tree, is used to tamp the tobacco in the bowl. The ritual of filling the Pipe signifies the joining of all the forces of nature: the creatures on earth and in the air, and man himself. The Pipe is to be used daily, and in every sacred ritual, to assure the blessings of Wakan Tanka, the Great Spirit. In prayers of the Sacred Pipe and in all other prayers, one ancient prayer is said, "Wakan Tanka onchimela ye oyate wakan wachin cha." ("Great Spirit, be merciful to me that my people may live.")

Their religious ceremonies were a living part of the Sioux social organization. As promised by the Buffalo Cow Woman, (giver of the Sacred Pipe), these rites were revealed by means of visions. The Pipe ceremony was incorporated into each ritual. The rites are essential in one's quest for maturity, wisdom, power. Thus did the people express their devotion to Wakan Tanka in a manner designed to fulfill their love for one another. Many of these rites are embodied in the Legends of the Lakota, as described herein. To bring understanding to the legends as well as to the religious beliefs and traditions of the Lakota, the principal sacred rites are described below.

Wiwanyag Wachipi, the Sun Dance. The Lakota Sun Dance, as practiced in ancient times and traditionally, requires the use of the Pipe many times. A candidate chooses his mentor; the Pipe is the intermediary. It is used to signalize the stages of rest on the journey to the chosen site of the Dance. The Pipe is used for blessing the tree, as well as throughout the traditional eight days required for preparing the Sun Dance. On the last day, the piercing of the candidates takes place. They dance until they have freed themselves from the tree, or until the day has ended. Each dancer has his own Pipe, which is placed on the Pipe rack at the altar. When the dancers wish to have a period of rest, one of the pipes is presented to the singers who sing throughout the days of the Sun Dance. Should the singers accept the proferred Pipe, the dancers may rest while the singers smoke the Pipe in the ritual manner. If the number of Pipes exceed the number of rest periods taken, the dancers must smoke the remaining Pipes when they retire to the sacred lodge. The Medicine man who presides at any particular Sun Dance, uses his Pipe to bless the tree, the arena, and to greet the morning sun each day.

Inipi, purification rite. This rite is an important proceeding before any religious ceremony, and before undertaking any vital event or project. A circular, dome-shaped structure is made from bent willow saplings and covered with robes. A round hole in the center of this lodge holds hot rocks, and on these rocks water is sprinkled mixed with sage. This creates a vapor. The steam creates perspiration in the human being, believed by the Lakota to contain impurities in the body, brought forth by the water spirits. Through the Inipi, the water spirits are brought forth, and the impurities are then washed off by plunging into a nearby stream, or by wiping the perspiration with sacred sage. Such purification rites are essential in order to directly communicate with Wakan Tanka. Before the Inipi, the leader conducts a ritual, invoking blessings on the proposed ceremony or task. The Pipe is smoked in a traditional manner. Even today the "sweat lodge" is used for purification before ceremonials.

The door to the lodge is opened three times. When it is opened on the third time, the assistant passes the tobacco-filled Pipe into the lodge, and all the Inipi participants smoke as it is passed clockwise around the circle. Each man prays as he smokes.

Hanblecheya, the Vision Quest. The prayer, or calling for a vision, was performed for various reasons. It is considered as a vital and important step on the road to maturity. Sometimes a man's fate was decided, if he happened to have a vision granting him the power to be a holy man, a healer, or a leader of his people. First, the Seeker of the Vision went through the Inipi ritual. Then he travels to the top of an isolated hill, carrying his Pipe. He prays there alone, usually for four days and nights. He remains naked, with only a bed of sage and a robe to ward off the chill of the night. The days are filled with constant prayer to the four cardinal directions, the Seeker walking with the Pipe extended, calling for a vision. At the end of the time specified for the ritual, the Seeker goes into the sacred lodge again, to smoke the Pipe with his assistant, joined by other wise elders who then interpret his vision.

If a vision is not evoked the first time, he can go back again and again in his quest. Women are allowed this rite also, but they choose a low hill or a protected valley. It is through this major ritual that the seven sacred rites were obtained traditionally. It is through Hanblecheya that holy men or healers receive their powers.

There are many Indian men even today, who undergo the Hanblecheya, seeking strength and wisdom to become a good man. His helper is a medicine man, and while he prays, this assistant stations himself nearby. The assistant may smoke many Pipes during the ordeal, praying always. But the initiate does not smoke his Pipe until he returns from the hill. Medicine men perform this ritual often, in order to renew their powers, or to seek guidance.

Keeping of the Soul. This rite entails cutting a lock of hair from one who had died, and keeping it in a sacred bundle, specially prepared for a period of one or more years. During this time the family and the band, as "Keepers of the Soul" are to live in an exemplary manner. At the end of the period, a feast is given for all the people, and the articles made or acquired during the year are given away to the people most in need. Then a ceremony ensues for the release of the soul of the loved one. The Pipe ceremony was part of the preparation of the sacred bundle, and the Release of the Soul ritual.

Hunkapi, the Making of Relatives. This rite is performed either between two individuals, or between two groups of people. A relationship is established, through this ceremony, which surpasses all other relationships. The bonds of those who are made "Hunka" are so strong that even death could not break them. Quite often, when one man died, his "Hunka" would undertake the responsibility for his wife and family. No sacrifice was too great for a relative acquired through the Hunkapi ceremony.

The Buffalo Ceremony, which Black Elk called "Ishna ta Awicha Lowan," ("Her alone they sing over"). The ceremony was revealed through a vision, just as all the other rites had been revealed. It is used to honor and purify a young girl when she reaches her menstrual age, the age of womanhood. The rite proclaims the girl a "sacred woman," who would bear sacred children. Her instructions, through this rite, exhort her to lead a worthy life and raise her children in the Lakota manner, so that they might be leaders of their people.

Tapa Wanka Yeyapi, Tossing of the Ball. This is a ceremony in which all the people may take part. A young girl, personification of the buffalo calf, throws a sacred ball made of buffalo hair and hide to the people assembled at the four quarters of a sacred circle. The ball is passed in the traditional way: west, north, east, and south. The one catching the ball returns it to the center each time. The fifth time, it was thrown into the air. Everyone has a chance to catch it then. The ball symbolizes the universe. Anyone catching it is believed to receive great blessing. After the game is over, the Pipe is lit and smoked. Or, it is touched by all. Those fortunate enough to have caught the ball receive special gifts. Then a great feast is given for all the people.

To reiterate, the Sacred Pipe is central to Lakota ritual and ceremony, prayer and blessing. The Pipes vary greatly in design. Some have stems with elaborate carvings, or are wrapped with porcupine quills, or covered with bead work. Some are quite simple. These are not for display, but are carefully cleaned and dismantled after each use and put away in a special pipe bag. There are individual Lakotas who use their Pipes daily. Some are practicing medicine men. Others may be plain people, ordinary individuals, those who retain a belief in the old religion and the power of the Pipe. Anyone may own a Pipe, and all Pipes are sacred if used for prayer. However, it is common practice and quite acceptable, to use a cigarette (usually hand rolled), to pray with, if one does not own a Pipe. The offering of tobacco is the important element in the ritual.

Many changes have occurred in Lakota religious practices. After all, time moves on, and man changes with time. So it is, with religious rites and ceremonies. Changes are introduced through the ages. But the Pipe ceremony is never omitted. Nor is it changed.

10

In all of its uses, it is the one symbol that remains constant.

Not all the ancient rites described here are still being practiced. Some died away because of United States Government interference with what the Christian believers called "heresy." Some have remained, despite having been forbidden time and again by the Bureau of Indian Affairs. Such a religious rite is the Sun Dance. The last Great Sun Dance of the Lakota was held in 1881, when the people were still bound in unity. For many years after that, the Sun Dance was prohibited by the United States Government. This was part of a policy to destroy Lakota religion and beliefs. Thus, ceremonies tending to preserve Indian identity, and hindering assimilation, were banned. In the 1930s, an attempt was made to revive the Sun Dance, in a dilute solution. The so-called "self torture," however, was forbidden. (One wonders when the self-torture of Catholic monks will be forbidden.) The Sun Dance reinforces Indian identity, develops unity, helps maintain Sioux tradition and beliefs. It is now seeing a great revival, and a renaissance of Sioux religious belief is occurring.

A more ludicrous attempt, although serious enough for the Sioux people, was the attempt of the United States Government to ban the "Keeping of the Soul" ceremony. This religious rite was banned by the government in 1890. On a certain day prescribed by law, all souls kept by the Sioux were ordered to be released.

There are many other religious practices and rites of the Sioux Nation. These vary from individual prayer rites, to the religious meetings and praying of the bands and families. Some Lakota have moved into the Christian religion, in varying denominations. But it is usually found that these people have made an accommodation to western beliefs; most retain some of their own racial beliefs and participate in the most important rites.

The difference in understanding of the religious meaning inherent in Lakota religious practices may be well expressed in the following incident: According to several men who had participated in a Sun Dance, whose who had been prepared by fasting, prayers, and blessing by the medicine man, ended their ceremony by lining up at the grounds. One by one the Indian Old People, Lakota who were present, and the non-Indian visitors, shook hands with the Sun Dancers, murmuring words of comfort to each as they passed. The Lakota Elders came through the line of dancers, pressed the hand of each, and said "Thank you." The non-Indians, in like manner, came to each dancer, took his hand, and murmured "Congratulations." That is the difference in belief, in values, and in understanding of the religion.

Man and the Black Hills

THE BLACK HILLS OF SOUTH DAKOTA, located in the southwest corner of the state, are part of the earth's great wonders. This marvelous natural formation is called *Paha Sapa* by the Lakota, and indeed the words mean "Black Hills."

Paha Sapa was Indian country from time immemorial. The Native Lakota saw these majestic hills as an altar where they worshipped their God. It is only natural, therefore, that through close association with the sacred place, and because of their spiritual devotion to the Hills, many legends have emerged, woven out of both fact and fiction.

The Lakota, or *Sioux* as they are more familiarly known today, have told and retold the legends from generation to generation. Some explain how the Black Hills came to be; another, how the Indian came to be. There are mystical as well as factual tales about the various places in the Hills. All are part of the legendry and the history of the Lakota. Excitingly narrated by a master storyteller, who had a respected and revered place in the Lakota society, the legends have substance as well as enchantment. We will try to translate some of these legends into the English language, as we heard them in our youth from the elders, and as we remember them in the frame of a modern society. An exact translation is of course impossible, for every language has its own flavor, its own meanings

13

and subtleties, and the language of the Lakota is one of the oldest in the world.

Many Lakota legends have much the same ring and imaginative ingenuity as the fairy tales of other peoples the world over. A liberal exercise of the imagination is the dominant ingredient in molding some of these legends. While many of them have no basis in science or fact, a historical and factual basis does exist for others.

The master storytellers, with keen memories and smooth tongues, held sway over their audiences, as they narrated their stories or histories before the flickering campfires. Their tales were told with song and gesture, in chant and mimicry. Some legends were amusing; others were serious; and some were much like lectures, or parables with moral implications. Those were the imaginative tales. But the Lakota documented his historical events, filing them away in a well-trained memory. These tales are called *wicho oyake,* "historical narratives."

First among the Lakota legends, is the story of the origin of man. We shall see, through Lakota legendry, how the Black Hills is intertwined in the very earliest days of the earth, with the origin of man himself.

"A long, long time ago," the Teller of Tales begins, *"Taku Wakan* (God, Holy Mystery), molded the Indian out of the clay of the earth." As he sits in the light of the flickering campfire, the Storyteller looks around at the eager young faces, smiles, and says, "I will tell you about this great thing. Have patience." Having gained their interest, he promises also, to tell how a multitude of animals, racing madly in a massive circle, caused the earth to burst open, resulting in the formation of the Black Hills. Thus it begins:

Lakota legends explain that Taku Wakan loved all things beautiful. The Lakota, in the beginning of time, was God's favorite creation because of his great beauty, his physical perfection. Now there was a time when Taku Wakan felt the urge to create a new creature who would have an intellect far above that of the many animals then roaming the earth. Before getting to work, Taku Wakan meditated, and determined, "He must be the master." He toiled long and carefully over a fire. With deft fingers He toyed with many varied figures. When a mold looked just right and appealing, He held it over the fire to give it solidity and color. Sometimes the molds came out pale or ashy white. If they were exposed to the fire too long, the molds emerged brown or even black. This did not please Taku Wakan. However, being a patient and tolerant God, He worked on.

14

One day, much to His delight, a mold came out of the fire with a tint and a luster most pleasing to look upon. Taku Wakan knew his work was done. Upon closer scrutiny, however, He saw there were no appendages upon his creature. To sustain a lust for life and to promise the continuation of life, He knew, there must be two of them properly equipped to propagate and continue the race. One creature must be the planter. The other, the hatcher. In just a little while, Taku Wakan made the necessary adjustments and tenderly blew into their lungs the breath of life. He named His master creations "Lakota." With a far-reaching arm He pointed to a beautiful land. "Henceforth this land shall be thine alone," He said. These lands were the Americas, as we know them now.

Taku Wakan surveyed His other creations. Though He knew them to be inferior, it was not in Him to destroy. And so to them He also gave the life-giving breath. He named them, and He placed them upon lands far, far away, with great waters between them and the Lakota. Thus were born the races of Man.

"As you know," the Teller of Tales began to explain,"the Black Hills is our church, our cathedral, the place held by the Lakota in reverent awe. Therefore," he said, "let us learn a little about this wondrous place."

In the repertoire of Indian folklore there are many legends explaining the origin of the Black Hills. Inching closer to the fire, the Storyteller promised, "I will tell you about one very famous legend, but first hear this."

The Storyteller now explained that, since the white man came, there is an idea that the Lakota were afraid of the Black Hills. "Not true," he said crisply and with a touch of annoyance. Later in life I came to learn that the Indian's reverence for the Black Hills is very much like the feeling many people on this earth have for the Holy Land, Jerusalem, Bethlehem, and Mount Calvary. Names and places like these stir religious emotions in devout people of the Christian faith. The Black Hills, in the same religious sense, affects the Indian in the same way. He had (and many continue even today) to have his own revealed religion. The Indian sought his God the best way he knew, and he found the Black Hills to be an ideal spot, where he pondered the mysteries of his being, and sought to prepare himself to lead a good life as a good man.

The Lakota worshipped in the Black Hills, ages before the white man came. Through this religious association he came to know every stream, the valleys, and from atop the craggy hills he knew awe when he viewed the breathtaking, panoramic land of the Black Hills, even as we see them now. With utmost devotion and

15

faith, the Lakota traversed the very center of the Black Hills. The absurd notion that thundergods, ghosts of ancestors, and evil spirits kept the Lakota from venturing into the very central part of the Black Hills is absurd.

There is little doubt that ancient man inhabited the Black Hills thousands of years ago. Here and there faint evidences of Man's footprints are found. His artifacts tell us that he was a thinking man. Weight rocks in ringed formations are found in the Hills and in the surrounding country. These rocks tell us that here, in this place, early man put up his dwellings, circular in shape, and used the rocks to hold them firmly in place upon the ground. Charred rocks in the center indicate the use of fire in those infant days of the earth. Near these *oti wota* (abandoned campsites) one may find white quartz pebbles in small piles, either in heaps or arranged in designs. Could it be that little children once played happily near those old campsites? One only speculates, and while mine is not an "educated guess," it is as good as any other. But it is no guess on my part, and many scientists now agree, that the Indian is a direct descendant of those ancient builders of their own unique civilization.

As the Teller of Tales rests a bit and gathers his thoughts together, let us think a little about the Black Hills and how they were created.

Some scientists theorize that these Black Hills were once the base of a giant mountain standing as high as fifteen miles in the air. Now only the granite stumps remain to tell a story of terrestrial convulsions that may have happened eons ago. The Hills are not as lofty nor as rugged as some other mountains, but it has been said they may well be among the oldest on earth. Perhaps the scholars can offer more plausible theories of the earth's behavior, to explain the scenic wonders and the awe-inspiring formations we see in the Black Hills. The geologist may explain what actually happened in this region, as well as in other places on the earth, in the vague and misty past. I like to think of it as part of the great story of life itself.

The earth in its youth was impetuous, even violent. Like all things young, it was addicted to explosive actions and sudden reactions. The Black Hills, showing no apparent relationship to other mountains, broke out on the surface of the earth. Were these great dome-like formations forced up gradually, by pressures from below, or were they born in pain and violence? Whatever it was that happened, there surely must have been chaos, confusion, and disorder. But time soothes and mellows all things. During a time scale that defies the imagination, this raw wound was healed, and human beings are now privileged to view with veneration the beauties of the

Black Hills.

We will not argue the merits of scientific theory versus Native beliefs and legendry. We do believe that the ancient explanations of the earth's beginnings, of man's beginnings, have a place of beauty in the history of man's thought. The legend explaining the creation of the Black Hills, however, is one that most stirs the imagination. This, then, is the story of the Big Race.

The legend of the Big Race belongs to the master Storyteller, and in a moment we will let him have his way. However, there is a curious and most interesting thing about the ancient legends of the Black Hills, which vary widely in thought and subject. On one point, however, there seems to be some unity of thought. All the legends, so far as I can remember, originally referred to the Black Hills as *Wita Paha*. These words mean *Island Hill*. The ancient inhabitants of this place were called *Wita Paha Tu,* meaning "Dwellers of the Island Hill." Why these old-time Lakota referred to the Black Hills as an island is open to conjecture. One theorizes that the Black Hills, isolated in the midst of vast, sea-like prairie lands which blend into shimmering, illusive lakes on a hot summer day, may have inspired such a name. Or perhaps the blue-black haziness of the Hills, as viewed from far away, may have given the Hills this name in times long past.

Let us return to the Storyteller, who surrenders to the earnest pleading of his young listeners by giving them the story of the Big Race:

Far back in the first sunrise of time (so say the legends), all the animals of the earth gathered here in the Black Hills for a big race. Here is how it happened and why it happened. At one time there were no Black Hills as we see them now. Only a vast prairie land existed, and upon it there roamed huge animals. There were flying vultures that preyed on the land animals. There were insects as big as eagles, with long sharp stingers that paralyzed and killed. The words *Unkche Ghila* in Lakota describe certain huge animals who once were numerous here, but are now extinct. These animals, oddly shaped and huge in size, roamed the land in great numbers. Then, for some unknown reason, they disappeared.

The words *Wichasha Akantu* designate Man, as distinguished from the animal and spirit world. This distinction—Man, Animal, Spirit, was needed because in that world of long ago man conversed freely with the animals and the spirits. In the midst of a world filled with predatory animals, in which man killed animals for food, and animals killed man, the idea came to man that there must be a way to bring order to such a chaotic world. He pondered long and

17

deeply upon the matter. Then one day he sent out a call to all the animals of the world to meet with him. A powwow was held. It was a memorable event because, in order to bring peace and order to the world, it was agreed that a race of immense magnitude was to be the solution. The race was to decide many things. It would result in sorting and separating the animals into their proper species by the smell of their bodies. It was to be a grand, epic feat of the ages.

Thus, to all *tatuya tona*, (wind flows or directions), messengers were sent, in order to announce the great event. These messengers were chosen from among the swiftest birds, and from among animals that could run like the flight of a strong arrow. Meantime, other animals were detailed to find suitable ground for a circular race track, and lay out a course wide enough and long enough so that the many animals who were expected could take part in the race. There were strict rules established, to insure a fair and orderly event. Every animal would have a chance, whether small or clumsy, weak or strong. Death was to be the penalty for any infraction of the rules in this race of the ages.

Since all sorts of animals appeared from every corner of the earth to take part in the race, heralders, in a common language, kept the newcomers informed of the rules. One rule established that once the race began, there was to be no stopping. All the racers must keep running, while the sun rose and set, one hundred times around the course. There were many guideposts, and the racers must run on the outer side of the markers. Stopping for food or water was at the runner's own peril. When the sun had risen and set for the one hundredth time, the judges would choose the winners.

As the day drew near for the big race, the land was covered with a seething mass of animals. There was great excitement, the racers all eager and impatient to be off and away. All were determined to be winners.

And then the fateful day arrived. A voice, unearthly and vibrant as thunder, shouted: "Hokane!" *Your fate is at hand!* The race was on. Instantly a mass of animals was on the move. The earth trembled under the impact of the stomping hooves. The race of the ages had begun; it was a test of endurance and sheer stamina.

Before the sun had set that first day, there were already groans of agony. The squeals and wailing of the weaker animals filled the air. They were trampled and crushed under the heavy hooves of the giant animals. The damp earth lost its moisture under the constant beating of hooves. Pulverized dust rose skyward, choking and obliterating the flying hordes of birds above, as they circled with the animal racers down below. High above, a bird would screech and then fall to the ground, a victim of weariness, or of some accident in the air.

After many days, the string of racers stretched into a continuous ribbon of animal flesh, the faster animals overtaking the slower runners. Now, like a giant wheel in motion, the racers fell into a wild, rhythmic stomping, like a massive dance as they raced round and round in the course. The earth shook. The air above vibrated. Animals brayed hysterically, crazed from hunger and fatigue. The din and stench was nauseating. But the race sped on like a giant serpent chasing its tail.

As the endless stream of racing animals moved madly on, lo and behold! The path of the racers sank crazily under their combined weight. Within the circle of racing animals a bulge appeared, strangely rising out of the ground. At first it was only a small mound. But suddenly, the earth quivered and groaned like a huge animal in pain. The mound rose faster and faster, and higher and higher. Then, with a thunderous roar, it burst open. Flames and dense smoke rose skyward, carrying fire and debris. Rock and ashes pelted the racers.

The animal racers lay dead in their tracks, covered with smoldering ashes and lava. The epic race of the ages ended in a *Wakipa* (a curse inflicted by the Great Spirit). So say the Lakota legends.

After the air had cleared and there was calm once more, within the rim of the circle of dead animals there was seen a pile of broken rocks standing majestically high in the air. The Lakota say this was how the Black Hills came to be. They called the mass of broken rocks *Paha Sapa*, or Black Hills.

Since the fabulous race of the ages was visited by a great holocaust, an act of displeasure by the gods, the winners were never fully determined. But legends say the lowly magpie was ahead of all the flying birds. And the *Unkche Ghila*, a huge animal whom no human being in modern times has ever seen alive, was leading the ground animals.

The Lakota say, that even to this day the remains of this ancient race track are still plainly visible, and there are many large bones still lying around along the historic track. The huge bones of the *Unkche Ghila*, which, once upon a time, roamed these prairie lands, can be found in the badlands to the east and south of the Black Hills.

There is a ledge-like row of hills surrounding the Black Hills proper. Within this row of hills, there is a depression or indentation which also encircles the Hills. The Lakota explain this is what remains of the racetrack upon which that fabulous race was run. But scientists explain these strange formations in a more practical way.

19

They are faults, or breaks in the crust of the earth, either shifting upward or dropping downward.

However that may be, the Teller of Tales says, "This is what happened in the long ago. This is the Lakota legend."

Here we leave the Teller of Tales, the master Keeper of the History. He has started us well on the way to the oft-told tales, the beloved memories of times past. The momentum is with us now, and I feel more secure in narrating, in the shadow of the respected Storyteller, those legends of the Lakota that were so much a part of my youthful life.

This is a Lakota sacred
chant, used in certain
ceremonies. The word
"Grandfather" signifies the
Great Spirit, or God.

A SACRED CHANT

Grandfather, behold me.
Grandfather, behold me.
I hold my pipe and offer it to you
That my people may live.

Grandfather, behold me.
Grandfather, behold me.
I give to You all these offerings,
That my people may live.

Grandfather, behold me.
Grandfather, behold me.
We who represent all the people,
Offer ourselves to You,
That we may live.

The Sacred Pipe

A LONG TIME AGO, FAR BACK in the most ancient times, a sacred pipe was brought to the Lakota people. It was a gift from *Taku Wakan*, and was presented by a *Ptesan Winyan*, (White Buffalo Woman). Along with the pipe, the strange woman also bestowed the laws by which the Lakota people were to live a moral life.

This memorable drama is regarded as a factual event. There were so many mystical aspects associated with it, that perhaps it should be treated as a legend, one vested with profound religious implications. This drama occurred in the misty past, when *wicasa akantu* (earth man) communed easily with the animal and the spirit world.

Of all the creatures of the earth, the buffalo was closest in affinity to man. Man depended on this one animal for his clothing, shelter and sustenance. Thus, man viewed the buffalo as a symbol in his daily thoughts, his dreams, his prayers and in his arts.

Now here is the tale of the Holy Pipe, as oftentimes called, and how the Lakota people acquired it:

A long time ago, from a large encampment of Lakota, two young friends, both strong and fine to look upon, decided to go on a hunt by themselves. So, taking their bows and arrows, they wandered far away over the rough terrain scouting for game.

The two men, though good friends, were opposites in na-

23

ture. One was impulsive, aggressive and uninhibited; the other was friendly and open-hearted, but quiet and reserved.

After roaming around awhile, they chose a high knoll upon which to rest and view the broad landscape. They could see many animal trails, all leading toward a full-flowing river some distance away. As they sat, leisurely scanning the rolling hills, they became aware of a moving object coming toward them at a slow trot, leaving a light trail of dust in the soft breeze. As it came nearer they saw that it was a lone buffalo, quite unusual, since buffaloes run together. On and on it came. Soon they saw it was a white buffalo cow, a very rare animal. "Must we kill it? We are taught that they are sacred. The Elders will be displeased," they said to one another.

Scrambling out of sight, they covered their bows and waited. Nothing happened. Stealthily they rose from their hiding place and there it was! What they saw was beyond belief. Instead of the white buffalo cow, there stood before them the most beautiful woman they had ever seen. She was immaculately dressed in the softest of buckskins, a headband circled her lovely hair from which white plumes swirled in the breeze. The young men stared in open admiration. The woman, sensing their feelings, was first to speak. "You with the human longing, come to me." The impulsive young man eagerly stepped forward and was about to embrace the woman when suddenly a vaporous whirlwind enveloped them. The other man, a brave though he was, stood unmoving, stirred by some strange feelings.

As suddenly as it had come, the fog and whirlwind disappeared. There upon the grass lay the young man, anguish upon his face, his bones exposed, as crawling worms attacked his flesh. Again the beautiful woman spoke: "It is the will of Taku Wakan that the male must lust after the female, but he also decrees that thinking man must exercise control. Your friend lives not by his mind but by his emotions; he now lies consumed in his own passions. You, being of sounder mind, will now act as my *Wahosi* (messenger). Return now to your people and tell your chieftain what you have witnessed and that I will be coming again, bearing a gift. A *Tipiyokihe* (two or more lodges joined together to provide ample space) must be erected so that many people can gather there; the event will be of lasting importance.

The woman then departed. The young man, still shaken, stole a sly glance at the place where the maid had stood. He saw a white cow buffalo trotting away. The young man's strange tale was not believed, until a party went to the scene and viewed the skeletal remains of his friend.

A big meeting house was erected, in obedience to the command given. The people anxiously waited, but nothing happened. The skeptics said the young man was demented, and the crowd became restless. Then an extremely unusual event occurred.

A *Tahinjila* (a light brown buffalo calf), apparently lost, wandered through the encampment, and as the young boys gleefully chased it all over, and just when they had it cornered, a startling thing happened. An apparition appeared. Instead of the buffalo calf, there stood a beautiful maid with a bundle upon her back. A deep hush fell upon the crowd.

The young man who was accused of being demented, knew who the beautiful woman was. He rushed forward, eagerly took her by the hand, and led her to the east opening of the large tipi. Once inside, there was complete silence except for the deep thunder roll on the heavy drums. She made formal bows to the chieftain and to the other dignitaries. In accordance with the preparations, in the center of the tipi there was a circle of hallowed ground covered over with sweet grasses, scented herbs and sage, all properly blessed by the medicine men.

Upon this hallowed ground the beautiful maid laid the bundle down. "This is a gift from Taku Wakan," she said. "At all times be aware of its mystic powers; henceforth humble yourself before it and be guided by its rules. It will always be your Maker." Unwrapping the bundle she displayed a long pipe. The bowl was of red stone. The long stem was of wood. Tied at the joint were twelve eagle feathers, all symbolic of products of the earth. (It has been said that the twelve feathers also represented the twelve moons of the year cycle.)

From the bundle she also took out a round stone. "This," she said, "represents the earth, your mother, with all its living creatures, its vegetation and its waters. It is as important as the pipe. Hold respect and at all times be conscious of your spawner."

She took a pinch of tobacco and stoked the pipe. From the perpetual fire she lit the pipe, took a strong draw and held the stem upward. There was a curl of thin smoke rising slowly skyward. "For you, Taku Wakan!" she declared. Then, in short, chanted prayers of invocation, she held the pipe by the bowl and with the stem she pointed to the four cardinal points of the earth, then once again upward, and then there was a deliberate pause, and then the stem was pointed downward to mother earth. "These are to be your revered gestures whenever you use the sacred pipe. Use it often. You will be happy people."

Now the woman carried the pipe to the chieftain and all

the dignitaries so they could draw upon it. As she did so, she explained the markings on the bowl. On the extended end of the bowl, there was a carving of a buffalo calf's head. "This means you must always venerate the fourlegs which inhabit the earth with you. Never take advantage or molest the mother with the young. The circles on the bowl, both large and small, are the symbols of rituals which you must henceforth practice as part of your lives. Taku Wakan will always answer your wants. Now I must go."

The *akicita* (order keepers) opened a way for her east-ward. The immaculate woman walked away with dignity, as the audience watched in awed silence.

After walking some distance, she sat down. When she arose, a transformation was seen. Once again there was a little brown calf trotting along. And then there was a series of changes: The little calf rolled over, and there arose a nearly mature calf. In turn the calf now changed into a fully mature cow. And then, before going out of sight, the people saw a shaggy, bony cow barely moving.

The men of wisdom interpreted the series of changes as the life-cycle of all living creatures of the earth. The happy innocence and carefree babyhood; the awakening and changes of adolescence; then the years of productivity. Lastly, the inevitability of aging, and the final return to mother earth.

So goes the legend, and thus did the sacred pipe come to the Lakota.

THE HOLY NUMBER FOUR

The Lakota consider all their activities, their prayers, and their lives, according to the number Four. This is because the four directions are recognized: the west, the north, the east, and the south. Time is in four divisions: the day, the night, the moon and the year. There are four parts in everything that grows from the earth: the roots, the stem, the leaves, and the fruit. There are four kinds of things that breathe: those that crawl, those that fly, those that walk on four legs, and those that walk on two legs.

There are four elements above the world: the sun, the moon, the sky, and the stars. Also, there are four kinds of gods: the great, the associates of the great, the gods below them, and the spiritkind. There are four periods in the life of a human being: babyhood, childhood, adulthood, and old age.

Mankind has four fingers on each hand, four toes on each foot, and the thumbs and great toes taken together form the sacred number Four as well. The Lakota believe, that since the Great Spirit has created everything in Fours, man should do all that he can in that increment, in the sacred number Four.

Milky Way and Fallen Star

ANCIENT PEOPLES THE WORLD OVER have been awed by the celestial wonders of the night skies. The Indian too, eyeing the endless expanse of stars twinkling like fireflies, searched for answers. He believed the luminous veil sweeping across the sky was the Trail of the Spirits, and the North Star was the father of Fallen Star, a supernatural being, the hero of many an Indian legend.

In the days when Indian life flourished upon unspoiled, well-protected prairies, and the animals roamed unmolested, Fallen Star symbolized the ideals of the Indian: honesty, courage, nobility, and brotherhood. He was the guardian of the red people against the hazards of nature. In times of misfortune, pestilence, and famine, he taught them the uses of medicinal herbs, and how to combat the diseases of nature. The Lakota people say that Fallen Star was especially kind to them because he was the son of a Lakota maid.

Tales of Fallen Star all point to the belief he was of celestial origin, a member of the *Maghpia Oyate,* (Cloud People). A belief still prevails that he now resides somewhere in the frosty dome of the heavens, a brilliant star, forever looking down with anxious concern upon his mortal and saddened people.

In ancient Indian life, there were men who specialized in the lore of the heavens. Intellectually gifted, with extraordinarily keen memories, these men studied solar behavior as well as the

29

faraway stars. They imparted their knowledge to posterity through oral narratives and by object lessons. They had knowledge of the fixed stars, the moving stars called planets, the visiting stars with tails and the sailing stars that sometimes loom into sudden brilliance and then fade in the deep blackness of the heavens.

The gradual whirling movement of the Big Dipper was part of their calendar. They made vivid and imaginative pictures of the star clusters. They said some of the clusters resembled animals of the earth. One cluster was called *Pa yamini pa,* (a monster with three heads).

After an evening of casual talk and story telling, it was the custom of the native people to go into the night, singly or in groups, attending to chores before retiring. At this time, if the sky was clear, the wise men who knew the stars gave lessons to the young, and to any others interested in the mysteries of the heavens. Pointing upward into the scintillating display of heavenly bodies, they traced out the animals portrayed by each cluster.

The ancient wise men said that all heavenly bodies exert influences upon life on earth, and the destinies of individual life are at all times under the spell of the sun, the moon, and the stars.

The Lakota people held in utmost reverence the most mystifying of all heavenly phenomena, the Milky Way. This mass of elongated, pale wonder of the sky held a definite meaning for them. They referred to the Milky Way, with great respect, as the pathway of the dead. This luminous trail, stretching from horizon to horizon through the dark skies and the cold expanse of space, was in their language *wanaghi tachanku,* (trail of the spirits). "It is the trail all Lakota people must take when fate overtakes them," was a common expression among the elders.

High in the heavens the Milky Way splits into two parts, one branch continuing endlessly across the sky. The other branch breaks off for a short distance and then fades away in a faint nebula. At this split in the Milky Way, Lakota legend says, there stands a Divine Arbiter of the souls of the dead.

Holding a plumed scepter in his arms, a token of his immortal authority, the Arbiter stood in judgment over the never-ending procession of ghostly marchers. Like death itself, there was no trail around the Arbiter. Judging each soul by the markings made by life itself, he searched for tattoo marks of the Societies to which the soul belonged. He looked for scars revealing the sins of human error. If a person showed such scars, the immortal judge pointed his scepter in the direction of the short trail, at the end of which was a precipice over which the ill-fated soul tumbled through space forever.

30

Those souls showing the markings of a moral life were directed toward the unbroken trail. This was a long, long trail, legends say, but at its end there was the *Wanaghiyata* (home of departed souls).

Wanaghiyata was the Lakota's conception of the hereafter. In this spirit world, only peace and plenty prevailed. The concept of their heaven was uncomplicated. Cool, fresh waters to drink, *Washecha* (foodstuffs aplenty), invigorating air to breathe, green foliage for shade, and lush grasses for the animals. Sickness, war, and death no longer marred the happiness of family life. Serenity prevailed. There were no pearly gates, or streets paved with gold.

Fallen Star was the fruit of a poignant romance, the tender tale of an earth girl and a strange young man who came from another world far in the heavens. The story begins:

Ages ago, in a small village of the Lakota, there lived a shy, comely maid, mild mannered and gentle. In her big black eyes there was always a hint of laughter. She had beautiful thick hair, immaculately braided with strips of soft, white fur. Skins of finest texture covered her dainty body. She was the very image of young, chaste womanhood.

From far and near, bold warriors came to woo this maid of the prairie lands where lilies bloom. The gallant men with strong, healthy bodies, wore their markings of prowess proudly and with dignity. It was most perplexing to make a choice from among such a group of warriors.

The courting ways of the red man were liberal. Sought-after maidens were closely chaperoned to insure only the best of unions, but all deserving braves had equal time to speak their words of love. These courting scenes usually took place under the light of an approving moon or near flickering campfires, where an elderly woman would sit, head discreetly bowed.

To *Tapun Shawin* (red-cheeked maid) there came one evening a young warrior, strangely radiant. With an aura of magic, he floated over the ground like a rolling fog. In the heavy moonlight, his shadow was crowned with a halo. When this young man, in the custom of the day, took his turn with the other suitors to speak his words of subtle persuasion, he won the heart of the maid.

As befitting occasions of this nature, it was joyously heralded to the village that Tapun Shawin was to be the bride of the charming stranger. While the mating rituals were in progress, the young man astounded the village by revealing that he was a member of the Maghpia Oyate and humbly asked the earth people to permit him to take his bride to a home far beyond the limits of the clouds.

31

And so the newly wed couple departed on their long journey, leaving the earth village in sadness. Arriving in the sky world, no sooner had they emerged from their bridal tipi than Starman's grandmother took over the management of the new household. She cast a stern eye upon the little earth bride, so young, so naive. Indeed she resented the intrusion. But she loved her grandson, and so, in a cold, methodical way, she began to teach the artless young bride the ways of the world above.

The earth girl enjoyed only the company of her man, and she accompanied him on many of his long, mysterious missions in the sky until one day she felt the stirrings of a new life within her.

It was now springtime in this strange land so far from the earth. In the warmth of the spring air, fresh grass carpeted the rolling hills with a greenish hue. Flowers burst into bloom, and the birds sang merrily as they tended to their annual springtime chores. It was the joyous season, the waking-up time for all living things. But alas, the warm sun and the feeling of being reborn sent twinges of nostalgia through the earth girl. To dispel the grip of sadness she wandered far away to the wooded hills, there to dream of her childhood. Vivid memories of her happy young life passed through her mind. These feelings gave way to the knowledge that she was uncomfortably heavy with the life within her. Feeling helpless and alone, she experienced an uncontrollable urge to do something reckless and daring.

The grandmother had been patient with the girl, knowing that women in her condition were not always rational. She had a fond hope that not too many moons away she would be holding a great-grandchild in her arms. But, with each day the young woman's behavior became more disturbing. She cautioned the girl to remember that the sky world was much different from the earth. Animals were more dangerous. Even growing plants and edible tubers could bring harm if not handled properly. The girl only sulked, and again wandered far into the hills, carrying her digging bar.

She remembered the many times she had gone as a small child to gather berries, herbs and tubers with her earth mother. As she rambled aimlessly here and there, recalling pleasurable childhood incidents, she spied a plant which she remembered as tasting bitter but pleasant. Casting aside precaution, she reasoned it would do no harm to enjoy once again the tangy taste of the plant she had once so enjoyed.

As she plunged her digging bar into the earth to extract the root, there was an unfamiliar hollow sound. As though plunged into quicksand, the bar crazily sank downward. She felt a queer sensation, as though the ground underneath her was crumbling away. Frightened, remembering now the warnings of the old woman, she reached out for something to grasp, but the movement only caused her to sink deeper, deeper, and then into oblivion.

When Starman learned what had happened to his cherished earth bride, a sadness beyond control overwhelmed him. Despondent and sullen, he refused solace and sought a remote spot in the sky to grieve and mourn his loss in solitude. To this day, so legends say, Starman sits with bowed head, never moving. This star that forever remains in one place is known to the Lakota as *Wazia Wichaghpi,* (North Star) or, sometimes *Wichaghpi Owanjihan* (the star always in one place).

The romance and marriage of Wazia Wichaghpi and Tapun Shawin had been short but idyllic. It had been a good omen for the Lakota because the child of this marriage, Fallen Star, would become their everlasting legacy. A headstrong girl, about to become a mother, had disappeared from the sky-world. But the strings of the legend extend back to earth, as we shall now see.

A group of small boys were hunting for rabbits one day, and for squirrels, turkey and other small game. Imitating their elders by stalking game through brush and thicket, they stumbled upon a most peculiar scene. For an instant they stood paralyzed in their tracks, then ran away screaming. Before going too far, however, fright gave way to curiosity. They cautiously returned for a closer look.

A woman, her comely face upturned, lay there as though in deep sleep, while a tiny child busily nursed from the breast of the motionless woman. Because the mother lay so unnaturally still, the boys picked up the baby boy, carefully wrapped him in calf-hide robes taken from their own shoulders, and took him back to the village. Breathlessly they told how they had come upon the scene, and how the newborn child had been vigorously nursing.

There was much curious speculation, but no explanation for this strange incident. Medicine men were apprehensive. What did it portend? Was she a cloud woman who had fallen to the earth? Many women, already mothers, came forward wanting the baby, but the elders of the village decreed that the child should go to a lonely woman in need of a child.

Now hunters brought fresh meat to the new mother and her adopted child, as custom decreed. The women in nearby lodges provided other nutritious foods. Everyone was solicitous for the welfare of the mysterious little boy.

He was named Fallen Star by the people. There seemed

to be no other explanation except that, like a wandering meteor, this woman with a child in her womb had fallen from the heavens, perhaps to bring blessings upon the earth people.

The young boy grew strong, nursing on a calf's bladder bag filled with nourishing, herb-flavored soups. He ate solids of pulverized meats prepared in concentrated mixtures seasoned with herbs and wild fruits.

Fallen Star was a most unusual child; he matured early into a sturdy, healthy boy. He played and hunted with other children, but he seemed to know he was no ordinary boy and was destined for special duties. Soon after attaining manhood, he told his adopted mother that his father was a bright star in the sky and by the command of Taku Wakan he must now watch over all the people of the earth. One night, quietly and mysteriously, Fallen Star left this earth, returning to the heavens of his father's people. But the Lakotas know he belongs in part to them, as the son of a Lakota mother.

Today, from somewhere near the Trail of the Spirits, known to others as Milky Way, Fallen Star sends rays of hope for his earth people.

Our young people today are
trying to learn the ways of
the elders. Many of them
feel the loss of their
traditions, their religion.
This yearning is expressed
in the poem of a young
Indian.

GRANDFATHER

Grandfather sings, I dance.
Grandfather speaks, I listen.
Now I sing, who will dance?
I speak, who will listen?

Grandfather hunts, I learn.
Grandfather fishes, I clean.
Now I hunt, who will learn?
I fish, who will clean?

Grandfather dies, I weep.
Grandfather buried, I am left alone.
When I am dead, who will cry?
When I am buried, who will be alone?

SHIRLEY CRAWFORD

Legends of Bear Butte

ALMOST DUE NORTH AND A LITTLE EAST of the city of Sturgis, South Dakota, there stands a solitary freak of nature called by the Lakota *Mato Paha,* (Bear Butte).

In the early days of white settlement this sharp mound was a famous landmark, a guidepost that directed the strangers who invaded this portion of the western wilderness. It was a beacon to the white wayfarers who braved the prairie lands to the east and the nearby Black Hills to the west. Military expeditions used it as the pivotal point in their operations. Today, this once famous mound, no longer useful, stands forgotten.

Before the white man came to this country, Bear Butte was even more important. It served as an altar for the Lakota, a stepping stone to the stars and the unknown. He made frequent pilgrimages to this mountain to say his prayers at its pinnacle and around its shoulders. In rigid soul-searching rituals he attempted to penetrate the veil of mystery, to look beyond, if possible, into the uncertainties of nature and find answers to the questions of life: infinity, whence we came, why, and whither we are going.

The Lakota call this sharp mound *Mato Paha* because, as told in their legends, a huge bear reposes underneath those steep shale slopes; his rhythmic breathing causing the oily shale to slide downward. Red philosophers say "Taku Wakan purposely caused this

37

strange formation so the red man might have an appropriate shrine upon which to pay him homage."

Geologists who study the earth's formations do not find anything unique in this sharp butte; similar formations are found elsewhere. Such formations are caused by hard, condensed cores of igneous rock working their way through the sedimentary strata of the earth's outer skin. Other learned men say these formations could be the stumps of once gigantic volcanoes.

Despite all scholarly explanations of the origin of Bear Butte, the Lakota have an altogether different version as to how the mountain came into being.

In the hazy sunrise of time, before man appeared, the animals of that primordial time were huge and ferocious. In that infant world there was the bear family, its members growing to enormous size, with shaggy fur and unsavory disposition. But the bears had enemies just as large, if not larger, with tempers just as obnoxious.

Thus one day in that ancient era of savage animals, a huge bear and an *Unkche Ghila* (dinosaur) met in mortal combat. The fierce battle raged for days and days, huge jaws snapping and sharp claws ripping at the flesh while labored breathing mingled with howls of pain. Legend says the monsters tore at each other so ferociously that rivulets of blood flowed down the gulleys. Finally, with a squeal of exhaustion and pain, the bear was forced to retreat.

Death was at his side as the bear crawled away to a lonely spot to hide from curious onlookers, to pout and lick its wounds in shame. As the beaten animal sat in a weary slump, strange things happened. The earth trembled. Fire belched from its bowels and ashes rushed down with devastating force. Water and mud spouted skyward, plunging the earth in darkness and chaos. And then, as swiftly as it came, the havoc ended and there was calm. The air cleared. Instead of the pouting bear, there was a sharp mound, high in the air, still smoldering.

Today this bear still sits in that very same position, sadly holding the secrets of limitless time, watching forever a changing world, a world that spawned a creature who can laugh and cry; an animal with a restless mind. This lonely mound commands large expanses of the country. Every day, upon its rugged contours, appear the imprints of nature's daily events. Will someone, someday, be able to decipher this journal of the ages?

From the lofty summit of this hill the all-encompassing view is marvelous to behold. There is a feeling of not being alone. Mato Paha had a firm grip on ancient man, as he searched for the why and wherefore of his being. Many tribes made long journeys to Bear Butte, seeking spiritual enlightenment. And around its base was the sacred terrain upon which those ancient peoples practiced their religion.

To gain some knowledge of himself, the red man made rigorous attempts to find a way to his Taku Wakan. One form of worship he practiced was known as *Hanblecheya,* the quest for a vision, or (more literally) a cry for a dream. In this ritual the worshipper, through solitary fasting and prolonged prayer, attempted to induce a vision by mental concentration. In gaining his vision he hoped to pierce the veil of mystery, pass into the realm of the unknown, and grasp some tangible proof that somewhere there is a domain of higher order where earth man goes after death.

Hanblecheya was practiced for other purposes, such as looking into the future, seeking aid in impending battles, and combating disease, but its purpose was chiefly for communion with Taku Wakan.

A person vowing to do the Hanblecheya first prepared himself through a series of rituals and consecration ceremonies. He was regaled and feted while being cleansed in mind and body. When deemed ready, he was led to some high mountain where he underwent his ordeal alone. For four days and four nights he prayed and fasted, exposing himself to the elements and other dangers. It was a solemn system of worship; he must forego food and water as well as any protective weapons.

History reveals that this sharp mound was popular with all vision seekers. The scope of vision, the dizzy height, sharp clarity of sound, and the clear view made it an ideal spot upon which to commune with Taku Wakan. Devoted seekers of spiritual knowledge felt that on this high mound they were nearer to realizing their dreams; there was a rapturous feeling of being projected into a visionary utopia.

Those of Christian belief have made pilgrimages to Jerusalem and the Holy Land. They tell of the joys, the trancelike raptures that filled them as they walked over the sacred grounds. The red man felt a similar devotional thrill as he prayed on the pinnacle of Mato Paha.

There are many legends of Bear Butte, but one has a special and tender meaning in the hearts of Lakota women. It is a tale of *Chekpa Oyate* (young children who make their home within the mountain). The Lakota have always believed that twins alone hold the secret to the processes of reincarnation.

The Lakota woman believed it was sacred to be blessed

with twins. Legend says there were special rituals for women who desired twins, because such children must come from Mato Paha. It was commonly believed that twins did not live long, blessing a marriage for only a little while and then, through death, returning to Bear Butte to reappear in another family at another time.

This faith in the Chekpa Oyate haunts the Lakota even in present times. They say caravans, when camped near Mato Paha, felt or even heard strange manifestations. Nostalgic sounds are heard of a long ago lively encampment, the echo of barking dogs, and then, in the twilight of the evening, the voices of little children, joyously at play, were distinctly audible. Those sounds of phantom children laughing and shouting tugged at the heartstrings, bringing tears to the eyes of Lakota women.

The red man believed that only little children hold the key to the meaning of life. Thus, it was traditional for young Lakota couples to make pilgrimages to Mato Paha, believing that if they mated near the sacred mound they would be blessed with twins who would choose them to be their next parents. For all newlyweds the soft buffalo grass at the base of Mato Paha offered a favorite mating ground.

Many strange and peculiar ornaments have been found in the pines by the Lakota, on the slopes of Mato Paha. Some carvings are of an intimate sexual nature. In those ancient times sexual relationships played a part in religious rituals. Hence the legendary belief that Bear Butte was the home of twins.

The Lakota traditionally treated freshly wedded couples reverently. A special bridal tipi was provided for them, pitched to the rear of the main circular encampment. Food and other essentials were provided for their comfort by special attendants; a woman relative usually did the honors. The Lakota always believed that mating was a sacred requisite of Taku Wakan; thus young people who were engaged in this life process were privileged to remain in seclusion until they voluntarily returned to practical daily life.

It was under such an ideal setting that a certain young couple prayed for twins. In their moments of physical ecstasy their minds focused on twin boys. In time, the young bride gave birth to beautiful boy twins, husky, healthy babies who had remarkably happy natures. For a few short years there was joy and happiness in this young family.

Serenity is not the main dish in life. For no apparent reason, one of the twins became violently ill. A medicine man was summoned, but he found the little boy already beyond any aid his medicines could give. There was sorrow in the lodge.

Tenderly the boy was dressed in his best doe-skin garments and laid on a high scaffold. Shrouded with him were bundles of extra moccasins and choice foods for his return journey to his home, Mato Paha.

For a time the grief was unbearable. The parents were heartbroken both for the dead and for the little boy who seemed lost without his brother. They dismantled their lodge and wandered far away over strange country.

Many moons later, when the world seemed less filled with the pain of their dead son, the parents turned their faces toward their homeland, Mato Paha.

Once home, the little boy seemed much happier. Gaily he ran over the familiar landmarks where he and his brother had played and dreamed great dreams.

The Lakota believed that twins would not live to maturity without each other, because they had been so closely entwined in mind and body. The young mother knew this, but hoped that in this case it would not happen. To bolster their hopes, the couple made special offerings to Taku Wakan, praying that their remaining boy would not be taken away from them.

Little children can sense the feelings of their parents, and the boy knew that his mother was not happy. With the wisdom of a grown man, he told his mother, strangely, "We must live out our lives as it is planned for us. I love you and much as I wish to remain with you, I owe a greater allegiance to my twin brother. He is lonely. Soon I must return to Mato Paha. Do not grieve, you will be blessed with other children."

One day, as he had predicted, the boy revealed that his spirit brother had come for him. The parents wanted to go with their son, but this could not be. They were still *wicha sha akantu* (mortal beings), who cannot enter the realm of the Shadow Land without the proper transitional changes. In his last moments, the boy was almost gay. He told how, in the land of the Chekpa Oyate they ride rabbits because they are *lusahun* (swift). My brother is now here with two rabbits, one for me, so now I must go," he said.

Thus, once again the young parents lost a son, true to the prophecies of the Lakota. But legend emphasizes that only the happiest memories remained with the parents, because they had given so much love to their twin boys.

Bear Butte was not only noted as a guidepost for early settlers, a sacred shrine for the Lakota, and a home of the Chekpa Oyate, it was famous for another thing. The Lakota say that, as far back as memory goes, this sharp mound served as a meeting ground for all the numerous bands of the Lakota Nation. *Oyate Kiwitaya,* (grand reunions of the peoples) were held here.

Periodically, all the Lakota from every part of their vast domain congregated here in mass meetings. The wisdom of every band was considered pertinent in all weighty problems, so the huge gatherings sometimes lasted many days and included general socializing. If urgent matters arose, emergency meetings were called.

The most recent congregation occurred in 1856, according to their winter count. This last grand reunion was urgent; it involved the momentous question concerning William S. Harney, a hated general in the United States Army. *Kasota* (annihilation) was the sentence passed upon him by the people gathered in this grand congregation.

Putinhin Skala, (White Beard), as Harney was known in friendlier days, had dropped low in the Lakota's estimation of him as a man of good character. He had lost all respect. Here, under the shadows of Mato Paha, he was marked for total destruction. The red man has always been subjected to unfair treatment; his trust in the white man had been repeatedly violated. Thus he was conditioned for almost anything, but what General Harney did at Ash Hollow on the Platte River was beyond forgetting. This act of infamy brought the Lakota Nation together, perhaps for the last time.

Because of the bitter resistance of the Lakota people, most early United States Army men had little affection for the Lakota warrior. However, some high ranking officers, honest at heart, played as fairly as they dared with the Indians. (Officers or agents who had feelings for the Indian were often either demoted or transferred.) General Custer was admired for his rough courage and despised for his ruthlessness. He was called *Pehin Hanska* (Long Hair), a *witantan,* (showy, prideful), a man with long yellow hair, of which he was inordinately proud. He should have been where women could admire him, but he chose the field of war because he was ambitious. The only road open at that time for ambitious military men was gunning down Indian women and children.

Another Army man was General Hugh L. Scott, who took a curious interest in the Lakota. A friendly man who studied their language, he took special interest in their sign language, the red man's universal form of communication. His scholarly interest won him an honored place in their hearts, and he was regarded as a true friend. Long afterward, General Scott regularly visited old Lakota friends on the reservation, where he spent many hours recalling old incidents by means of the sign language.

The Lakota had high regard for protocol. In matters of

diplomacy, reserve and dignity were the rules of conduct. He was puzzled by the abominable tempers some high ranking military men displayed in meetings, and the insolent pride they had in their tempers and bad manners. The Lakota respected some officers for their honesty and ignored others for their cowardice and childish behavior.

There were some who were despised for their treachery, such as William S. Harney. Colonel Custer belonged in this category also.

Tiapa wichakte is a Lakota phrase meaning "slaughtered in their tipis," an atrocity in which innocent women, children, the sick, and the maimed, were attacked and murdered in the tipis. This happened when warriors were away from home.

In the year 1855, General Harney, boasting that he would subdue the Lakota, moved out of Fort Leavenworth, Kansas, with his officers and a contingent of one thousand soldiers. He marched in a southwesterly direction along the Oregon Trail. In the course of his march, he came upon an encampment of Lakota at a place known as Ash Hollow along the Platte River. The Lakota, under the leadership of Little Thunder, were peaceful Indians. There were no hostilities in the southern portions of the Sioux domain at that time. All the war-like acts, disputes and skirmishes were in and around the Black Hills and in the northern hunting grounds.

General Harney made friendly overtures, and Little Thunder agreed to meet him in an amiable parley. While the General and Chief Little Thunder were engaged in talk, the general, secretly deployed his soldiers, who completely encircled the encampment. After the trap was set, and the people killed, Harney disdainfully told Little Thunder to go and defend his people. A massacre occurred that ranks high among many atrocities suffered by the red man in which women and children were the victims. Harney acquired uncomplimentary names such as *Wichayajipa,* (wasp) and *Ohunkeshni tokawichaya,* (one who plunders or rapes the weakest of the people).

At this last reunion, the Lakota held mass prayers, asking Taku Wakan to help them avenge the shameful slaughter of Ash Hollow. Many an old timer expressed regret that General Harney was not in Sheridan's campaign.

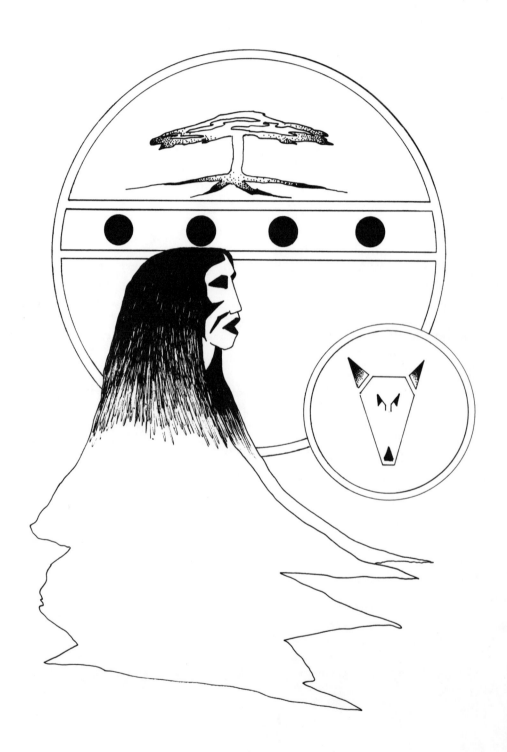

Warm Waters

K NOWN TO THE LAKOTA AS THE LAND OF WARM WA-
TERS, the southern portions of the Black Hills
have always been closely linked with lore and romance. This virtual dreamland of enchanted terrain and scented atmosphere has remained unchanged through the ages. The Lakota
say these lands belonged to the "underground people," highly intelligent beings with supernatural powers, who inhabited subterranean
lands, much like those who occupied infernal lands in ancient Greek
mythology. Legends say these people bred game animals for human
consumption and kept perpetual fires ablaze to heat the waters that
flow up to the surface, thus keeping the flowers in bloom and the
medicinal shrubs growing the year round.

At one time the Lakota saw the Black Hills as an island.
He still refers to the Black Hills as an island. In these hills and in the
canyons of the warm, gushing waters, ancient man has left a story,
not written in words, but a story nevertheless, of his sojourn here.
While he lived, he made drawings on rock walls for us to decipher. He
mined flint for his implements. He left weight rocks in circles to let
us know he lived in circular lodges. In the red man's search for
answers to a mysterious life, many tales were born. Some of the
legends say those underground dwellers held the Lakota in high
esteem because many years ago a young Lakota brave married a
princess of the underground world.

The lands nourished by the warm waters were fertile places of great value. Sweet smelling peppermint plants and pulpy rosebuds for tea abounded here. A profuse growth of medicinal herbs and leafy greens for soups, and many kinds of edible tubers thrived around those areas. The open warm water streams attracted water fowl and other game animals the year round. The Lakota say these oasis-like places were gifts of Taku Wakan, and they cleansed themselves in the mineral pools and drank the saline waters to maintain their health. They gave the name of *Mini awoblu makoche* (land of bubbling waters), to this part of the Black Hills, and they cared for it well. Around this bewitchingly beautiful region the Lakotas wove their tales of fact and fancy, leaving an oral history and a classic literature to enrich man's mind and spirit.

The eagle who lives in the Black Hills was glorified in many legends. He represented agility, grace, and strength. It was he, not the owl, who had wisdom. He alone flew so high that he had a panoramic view of Mother Earth. Thus, his judgment was believed to be unerring. It was a bad omen and a sin to kill an eagle, but men dared to trap him because his feathers were needed in sacred rituals. The trappers of eagles vowed they heard him in song as he soared high in the blue sky, his lyrics foretelling events, both good and bad. Eagle songs are still sung by medicine men as a nostalgic return to an era that once was.

The Lakota believed that the spirits of ancient peoples who inhabited the Black Hills in the dim past manifested themselves on occasion in bonfire rituals. Such ghostly festivities could be observed at certain times and places, legends say. Bonfires, brilliantly lighting secluded spots, showed ancient revelers jubilantly engaging in games of chance, lively dances, feasts, and commemorations of past glories.

These night scenes were baffling, for when curious observers attempted a closer view, the whole scene of phantom revelers would grow dim and fade away like a ghostly phosphorescent glow. The fires would die out, and only the echoes of the rhythmic beat of the drums and the faint voices of the singers would be audible in the darkness of night. Day time inspection of the bonfire spectacles almost always revealed artifacts, confirming the existence of an ancient people.

Magicians in ancient times gathered here periodically to display their magic, because these warm waters were held to be sacred and mystical. The medicine men practiced their skills in contests with their fellow magicians, competing for high honors. Often a temporary truce was decreed, so that holy men of other tribes might attend the meetings with immunity. As in modern-day conferences of learned men, the Indian mystics would meet to exchange ideas, and the uses of new herbs were demonstrated. The holy men had strict rules of behavior and accorded each other the most profound respect. When in session, they sat in a circle with their gear in front of them, including holy bags, gourds and other charms necessary to their profession. No other hands were allowed to touch them. In such meetings, it is said, the holy men competed for high stakes. True or false, some of the deeds performed must have been really astounding.

The tales of such meetings are many, but the following is best remembered. Despite the solemnity and the rigid codes of conduct, in this case some humor may be detected.

Such a contest was in session long ago. There were the *Yuwipi* (in wraps), escape artists who claimed they could free themselves no matter how securely they were bound, because they had invisible helpers. There were the keepers of the *Inyan hokshila* (pebble boys), who said that with the help of small pebbles they could find lost objects or trace a missing person. Suction artists were there too, who claimed their magic sucking power could draw out deeply embedded spear heads or stubborn infections anywhere in the body, an art believed to be effective in saving lives.

There were also the voice throwers and the spell-casters, men skilled in ventriloquism and hypnotism, who generally practiced their art to amuse the public, but also at times for sinister purposes. So it is said.

Usually, some novices were allowed to display their skill with a few mild tricks, and then, as the session progressed, the tricks became more mystifying. Strange voices could be heard, while gourds rattled and bounced about, seemingly without aid. Spectators, especially the skeptics and the scoffers, were pelted with invisible objects.

With more sophisticated trickery, a holy man intoned a prolonged poetic chant. When he paused, from his throat, like a toy cuckoo, came a curlew's melodious call giving warning of an impending storm. It was so real that some actually thought they saw the bird, and the drummers banged a roll on the tom-toms in approval.

Another magician, rising to his feet, also chanted magic poetry, appealing to invisible helpers that water was needed. In step with the rhythm of drums, he performed a stomp dance, bouncing around gingerly in a gyrating movement and then, in a climactic leap, coming down hard upon the ground. There before the skeptical crowd, a fountain of water spurted high into the air. The crowd surged forward for a closer look, and then burst into cheers. The deed was certainly baffling!

47

A third man came forward with a pipe. A staccato monotone flowed from his lips as he stoked the pipe with magic tobacco. His monologue conveyed to his fellow magicians that they must enjoy the soothing pipe with him. Lighting the pipe, he inhaled deeply. When he exhaled, blue flames hissed from his mouth and nostrils. He attempted to pass the pipe around, but his disgruntled fellows all refused the proferred pipe. Since it was the most mystifying trick, the spectators clamored for more, shouting derisive epithets at the other contestants.

The shouting died immediately as a stranger appeared. Who he was, where he came from, no one knew. He stepped inside the circle of performers, a deliberate discourtesy. Clumsily he dragged his feet over holy bags, trampled on gourds and other magic gear, causing a general uproar of displeasure among the holy men. "Huwa haha," they said, signifying that they had been subjected to utmost indignities.

Unmindful of their loud grumblings, the stranger removed one of his moccasins and tossed it to the entranceway.

As it hit the ground, a screech owl appeared, twisting its head around at the circle of men. When all had seen the queer little bird, the stranger took off his other moccasin and toppled the owl. Two moccasins lay where the owl had stood.

The stranger paused, eyeing his fellow magicians in disgust. Chanting a monologue, he removed a string of colored beads from his neck and held them gently in his cupped hands, whispering magic words upon them. Suddenly he slammed the beads to the ground. The startled group sat straight up, bristling with expectation. A rattlesnake lay where the beads had hit the ground, its tail giving off a deadly sound as it reared its ugly head and slithered in front of the circle of bewildered holy men, its black tongue leaping out menacingly at them. The holy men forgot about their magical powers and made themselves as small possible behind their bags. The evil snake made extra leaps at those who appeared to be most frightened. When the snake had made the circle, leaving the magicians limp, the stranger waved a feathered wand. There lay a string of harmless beads.

He was not finished. Now he took bits of food from his bag which he passed around. Before anyone had tasted the food, he raised a warning hand and sang: To you who deceive, this food is death." Many magicians did eat the food, but did not die, because according to the legend, this was only a practical joke of the great magician.

THE CIRCLE OF LIFE

The circle is sacred, the Lakota believe, because Taku Wakan caused everything in nature to be round except the element stone. Stone is the instrument of destruction.

The sun and sky, earth and moon are round. The sky is deep like a bowl. Everything is round that breathes like the body of a human being. Things that grow from the ground are round like the stem of a plant. Thus, man should look upon the Circle as sacred. It is the symbol of the circle that marks the edge of the world, and therefore of the four winds that travel there. It is also the symbol of the year.

The day, the night, and the moon go in a circle above the sky. Therefore the circle is a symbol of these divisions of time. It is the symbol of all time throughout creation.

The Lakota make their tipis circular. Their camp is circular. They sit in a circle in all ceremonies. A circle that is made for an ornament, undivided in any way, is understood as the symbol of the world and of time itself. If the circle is filled with red, it designates the sun; if with blue, it designates the sky. Should the circle be divided into four parts, it signifies the four winds. If one divides the circle into more than four parts, it symbolizes a vision.

The mouth of a pipe should always be moved in a circle before the pipe is formally smoked. The traditional Lakota, in times long past, firmly believed these things, and many still do.

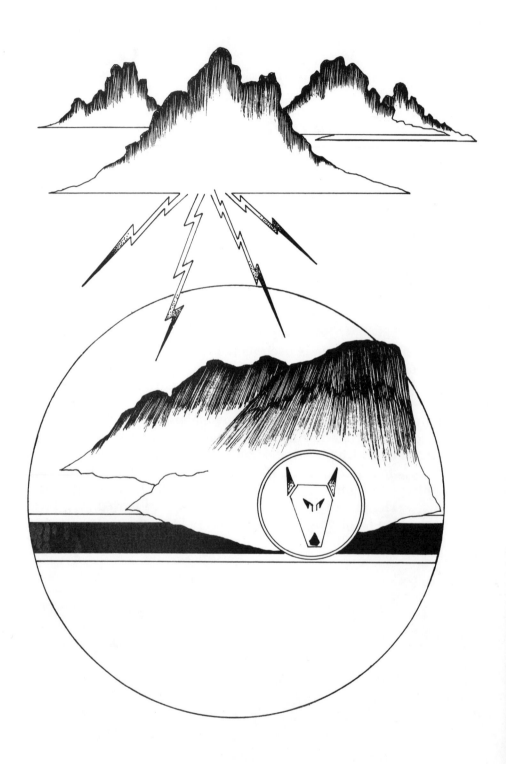

Red Canyon

IN THE SOUTHWESTERN EDGE OF THE BLACK HILLS of South Dakota, there is a little town called Edgemont. Running directly north from this town, a valley hugs the western edge of the Black Hills. It is called Red Canyon. The Lakota people say this canyon is part of the race track on which, once upon a time, hordes of animals competed in a fabulous race of the ages.

The cliffs on each side of the canyon are high and steep with broken jagged rocks. In a true sense, Red Canyon is not a canyon at all, but a wide valley hemmed in by walls of rock. In the northern part of the valley the bluffs are of pure red sandstone capped with layers of white rock, giving them the appearance of berry pies topped with whipped cream.

Along this valley there are many ruins, indicating that in early history there may have been considerable human activity. Pieces of bulky machinery lay abandoned, the remains of the white man's one-time mining operations. There are also ruins of what might once have been ranch spreads, or even garrisons, now rotting away.

Years ago, the Cheyenne stage coach from Wyoming to Deadwood, South Dakota, made its regular dusty trip through this valley. As with all old pioneer trails, this one trail had its tales of depredations, stage holdups, and killings; tales of the hectic days of the old West, full of crime and conflict. These tales of white men's activities are only a part of recent history.

The valley is rich in ancient lore; it harbors the remains of a misty era. The red man who lived in this land for ages has left the legends of his people, who lived here thousands of years ago, and the marks of their sojourn are clearly evident.

In the legends of the Lakota, these ancient people are regarded as super-humans who purposely left their artifacts scattered here and there as gifts of their culture, so that the red man might learn something of his ancestors. These objects are a source of endless wonder to the Lakota.

Inyan Owapi is a Lakota phrase meaning "rock writing" or "stone inscribing." On the walls of Red Canyon there are a few such inscriptions. And, as might be expected, the Indian has authored many imaginative tales as to who may have done the etched writing, how long ago, and why.

The Indian knew about the hieroglyphic stone writing in Red Canyon and elsewhere in the Black Hills. He said that ancient peoples of considerable intelligence made the writings. Their meaning? He did not worry about it because unexplainable things belong only to Taku Wakan, and only after death can full knowledge of all life's mysteries be revealed.

In Indian life, medicine men were held in awe and respect. One reason was that they were believed to have power to cast spells and bewitch people. They were indispensable, however, because they alone had knowledge of the mysteries of life and they alone could sing the ritual songs. In tempo with the beating of the drums, they chanted and called out the messages conveyed in the figures inscribed on the rock walls.

The Lakota say the actual writings were made only at night, a belief that added to the mystery surrounding the artists. Many a night watchmen took turns to catch a glimpse of the carvers, but never with success.

However, in Lakota legends, it is said that those mysterious artists have been seen. One legend credits the *Wakan Gli* (lightning), because after a severe lightning storm, bluish sheets of fire could be seen clinging to the stone cliffs, and when the sparks faded, newly carved figures could be observed. In another legend, vultures with sharp beaks clung to the stone walls like huge bats, and when they flew away, new figures had appeared. Still other legends say that in ancient time there were man-birds, who hovered like humming birds near stone walls, carving out forms of animals and other signs. However, one story seems to have most credence. In the eerie blackness of night, the faint voices of ghostly mourners, wailing premonitions, and those of departed braves singing a war chant once blended with the moaning of pine trees. Those were the true omens revealing that messages from *Wanaghiyata* (spirit world) had been carved on the stone walls. It was deemed wise for mortals to take heed and read the signs, paying homage to their ancient ones.

Despite the fact that Red Canyon is now serenely quiet, serving only as a cattle range, many signs indicate that once upon a time, in the distant past, a civilization of high order flourished in this valley. Carved pictures, pottery, and flint quarries only hint at what may have taken place here thousands of years ago. One thing is certain. These ancient peoples were the ancestors of the present American Indians.

The Lakota people of long ago held great periodic reunions. A gathering of such magnitude was called *Oyate Kiwitaya*, (regrouping of the bands). When the master minds of the Lakota decided to call such a gathering, runners were dispatched to all bands of the Nation to apprise them of the coming event. They had no calendars, but they had other methods of determining time, such as the phases of the moon, the position of the Big Dipper in the sky, the mating of animals, and the ripening of berries in certain areas of the land. These and other methods were used in setting time; the errors in days were negligible. They held their gatherings on schedule.

At these gatherings, chieftains and headmen of the various bands discussed matters of politics, questions of unity, and the promotion of a strong nation. Current ideas and fashions were exchanged. Varied societies met in nationwide social functions. The young displayed their strength and skill in games and contests where partisan rooters wagered heavily on their favorite competitors. Medicine men met in contests of magic. New herbs were discussed, and the latest in healing methods was demonstrated. But the matter having priority was the love life of the young. The people believed that inbreeding was a curse. They said children of close blood ties were weak and prone to diseases of the mind and body.

Thus, young girls were encouraged to welcome the courtship of young men from other bands. Marrying into another band was a social achievement. It brought recognition and prestige to the bride. It was followed by a round of social affairs and many gifts.

At such a mass gathering long ago, a young man from the far north country courted a maid from the southland. Without warning, the playful experimenting of two freshly ripened young people suddenly burst into a flaming passion of love. They were caught in a web that knew no reason. The young woman was from a long line of great chieftains. She was jealously guarded. No opportunity was

53

given to assuage the fierce yearning they had for each other.

The maid's chief declared that the young man was immature and lacked accomplishment. If he wished to be considered as a suitor, he must prove his worth in the hunt and on the field of battle. He must win decorations for his coup-stick and be publicly acclaimed as a warrior and hunter. In plain words, the young man was unworthy of the daughter of the southland, said the chief.

The young boy's kin were ordinary people perhaps, but they were proud. They retorted that the girl did not display true love, but only female passion which above all needs fulfillment and is not choosy. Thus, males fight and sometimes kill each other because of such lustful females. Their son should not be the victim of such a designing young female, they declared.

Thus were the orderly processes of the laws of nature rudely interrupted. There were tears and sadness when the two young people took leave of each other. The man was gently admonished that he was much too young for serious thoughts of love; he should be grateful for narrowly escaping the wiles of a predatory woman. And so he tried to forget, but sadness followed him.

At night he wandered to the hilltops and there he searched the luminous face of the moon for solace. He knew that the maid too sought hope and comfort in the kindly moon. He sang songs of love and sent messages through the all-seeing rays of the genial moon.

Then one day he knew that he must go to the southland. He felt she was calling to him. Come what may, he must go to her though many dangers lay ahead. His parents received his tragic decision with understanding, and his plan to make the long journey was announced to the village.

His friends and relatives made weapons and prepared food for him to take on his hazardous journey. Moccasins were made from the toughest of shrunk hides, his quivers were filled with the finest arrows. *Wasna na Wakapapi* (concentrated foods with fruit preservative), nourishing and sustaining, were among the gifts from his village people.

When all was ready, he took leave of his parents, perhaps never to see them again. A brief ceremony of farewell was held, then an escort of young friends accompanied him, singing light-hearted songs as they marched away. At night-fall his friends bade him a final farewell. Now he must face the hazards of the long journey alone.

For days he kept up a brisk pace, jogging steadily for long distances. When tired, he slowed to a walk or climbed a hill to scan the landscape as a measure of caution. He ate sparingly of his food; the southland was far, far away.

One day, after many sleeps, he sensed that someone was stalking his trail; he feared that soon he might be surrounded and captured. To avoid this danger, he made a hasty retreat toward a high, craggy mound. The enemy was now openly in hot pursuit. From atop the mound, his arrows had much more force than those of the enemy, which were coming upward, and for days he was able to hold them off. Although they crawled up the steep sides to catch him asleep, he was ready for them in the darkness of night, and silently he slew the prowlers.

After many days of the siege, his bladder water bags were empty, his food sacks were depleted, and only a few arrows were left. It was time for action, so he made his plans and prayed. With the approaching darkness a vicious storm suddenly blew in. While the thunder rumbled loudly and dumped blinding sheets of water upon his distracted foe, he fled unharmed past their cordon.

Thirst, hunger, and lack of sleep assailed him, but the thought of capture spurred him to extraordinary exertions, running and sometimes stumbling in the dark. Finally he fell exhausted near a clump of high rocks. He was now quite safe, and he crawled into a crevice. There he fell into a deep coma.

How long he lay in that death-like sleep he did not know, but it was night when strange noises awakened him from his slumber. Accompanied by flashes of light, they came from a rock wall. The night air was abuzz with flying bits of rock, a weird spectacle in the darkness. He was frightened. But soon, as though in a dream, a friendly voice soothed away his misgivings: "On the morrow there will be a sign upon the rock wall. Abide by the markings," said the mysterious voice.

In the morning, a warm sun was shining and he felt rested, his mind much clearer. But that eerie dream, the noises, the sparks, and that unearthly voice, would not go away. Filled with curiosity, he looked toward the stone wall, and there it was! As the voice had said, there were some strange carvings. Clearly, as if by some magic inner perception, he knew their meaning. They told him that foxes would come to his rescue and protect him, but he must lie in wait until dusk. Though he had no weapons, no food, and no water, the youth was now calm. When night came, in the luminescence of the moon he saw a fox on the crest of a nearby hill. It yelped mournfully as though transmitting a special message. Soon other foxes appeared. They were to be his escort and protectors on the remainder of his journey to the southland.

He watched in the growing darkness as the fox pack gathered. When all had assembled, they came for him. At the command of the leader fox he staggered painfully to his feet and followed the pack as they slowly and silently ambled away in the darkness.

First they took him to a water hole, where he threw himself down and put his mouth into the cool, soothing spring water. He bathed his face and doused his head to revive his spirits. He was now ready for the long march. The leader fox, with sharp, unerring eyes, went ahead while the other foxes formed a protective cordon around him.

In keeping with the instinctive habits of the fox, marching and other activities were done in the darkness of night. During the day he was cleverly concealed in crevices or under thickets and was kept warm and comfortable by their furry bodies. Every precaution was observed to keep him safe from all possible enemies. Liver and kidney from freshly killed young deer and buffalo calves were his main sustenance. The journey was long and arduous but the foxes, faithful to the written commands of *Inyan Owapi* (rock writing), guarded him well.

One day, after what seemed an interminable time, they sighted a large village. As they neared it, the foxes slowed their pace, allowing the young man to advance. Somehow, the young man felt lost and alone. On the long journey the foxes had become trusted friends. He would miss them. Far back on a sharp knoll they sat on their haunches, watching and waiting.

An early dawn scout making his morning tour spied the young man sitting forlornly on a hilltop. As was the custom, the scout approached, informing the young man by signs that he was a welcome guest of the village. The foxes, seeing their mission had come at an end, yelped a mournful call and scampered away over the horizon, never to be seen again.

The young man was escorted to the *Tipi Iyokihe* (council lodge) of the village, where the elders sat in quiet meditation. He was greeted with the ritual of the pipe and requested to sit at the far rear of the lodge, a place reserved for all honored guests.

After the brief ceremony, the young man was given the honor to be heard. Calmly and directly he made known the purpose of his long journey. He recounted the harrowing experiences of his journey, the long siege on the craggy hill, his miraculous rescue by the thundergods, the revelations of the *inyan owapi,* and how the faithful foxes guarded and guided him to the southland and to this village.

The elders, after long deliberation, avowed that the

young man's long journey, with its many harrowing experiences, was indeed a most commendable and remarkable feat. Henceforth, he should be an honorary member of the stout-hearted society.

Legend says that the young maid had remained faithful to the youth and had never married. Her family withdrew its barriers, and their lives were joined. In time, they were the parents of many a stalwart son.

In later life, the Fox Man, as he was known, became a renowned medicine man. And, as in many cases in the social structure of the Indian, he founded the Fox Society, a way of life which is still practiced.

This social order of the Fox exists in many tribes of the Plains. Its members dedicate themselves to a life of service and self-denial. Their pledge was: First in war and in the hunt. Be helpful wherever you may be. *Wowachinye* (be helpful always) was their watchword.

The brisk and hearty songs of the Fox Society can still be heard in Indian communities, and the influence of this charitable order remains alive to this day.

So it is said, and so in truth it is.

Thunderhead Mountains

IN THE SOUTHCENTRAL AREA OF THE BLACK HILLS there is a series of grayish granite out-croppings. They are not jagged and sharply pointed like the Needles farther north. Rather, they are blunt and rounded, like bubbling thunderheads peeping over the horizon. These gray rocks were known to the Lakota as *Wakinyan hinapa Paha* (Hills like Thunderclouds).

The Lakota believed the Black Hills to be the home of the mighty thunder. Because, regardless of the observer's location, if the Black Hills were visible, the inevitable thunderheads always bubbled skyward. It was not pleasant to be under those cumulus clouds as they formed into massive, electrically charged thunderheads. Deep, low rumblings were often heard, the legends say. They were the angry threats of the thunder gods as the dark clouds expanded into towering thunderheads. When the loose hair on the head reached up toward the clouds it was a sign that the storm would be vicious, and shelter must then be sought.

The Indian, awed by thunderstorms, knew the storms brought rains that refreshed the air and revived life and vegetation. It was a necessity for all living things. What he found difficult to understand was that sometimes the storms became violent, even causing death. He knew he must live with these unpredictable elements, so he compromised by making frequent *Waunyan* (sacrificials). Through the summer months he appeased the wrathful thunder gods with prayers and rituals of supplication. With his offerings to the Giver of *Mah Aju* (dew or rain on plants), his plea was that no harm come with the storm.

Heyoka Woze was an ancient thunder ritual handed down from the misty past. Medicine men of other faiths have ridiculed the thunder ritual as crude and lacking in dignity. However, the thunder dreamers defend their practices as legitimate, within the bounds of propriety. Further, their rituals were the dictums of a vengeful god and they had to be obeyed. To evade them meant death.

The word *Heyoka* designates a clown. *Woze* is a verb form describing the act of retrieving.

The ritual of the Heyoka Woze, like walking on hot coals in bare feet or lying down on sharp nails, challenged the normal laws of nature. But in this ritual, an air of comedy pervaded the performance. In a grotesque costume, the thunder dreamer acted out his dream. His face, marked in hideous fashion, displaying the antics of a clown, he attempted to amuse the spectators with capers and witty observations, always reversing the sequences of action. It was a routine of wit and comedy, but beneath it all there was an intense ritual to a relentless god.

Women thunder dreamers followed a similar routine, but legends say the thunder gods decreed that female dreamers had to perform the Heyoka Woze in complete nudity. Women performers were allowed only a minimum of decorative ornaments and wore in their hair floating tail plumes of the *Anukasun* (bald eagle) which also holds a mystic place in the legends of the Indian. The white plume is the symbol of flexibility and swiftness, like lightning. The ankle part of their moccasins was trimmed with fine fur. Their long black tresses, usually gathered in a tight roll, dangled over the left eye. Lightning struck many a shy maiden, legends say, because virginal modesty restrained her from performing the ritual in the nude.

In the dramatic climax of a thunder ritual the performer, in tempo with the staccato beating of a drum and poetic chanting, approached a steaming kettle in a twisting, leaping dance. Cued by the banging drum, he would plunge his bare hand into the steaming kettle and yank out choice edibles, which he handed to honored guests and medicine men seated in a semi-circle. The stories say that because the dreamers performed their ritual with gusto, and had implicit faith in the mysticism, the scalding liquids had no ill effects on their hands.

Wakinyan is derived from another Lakota word meaning to refresh or to revive. Thus, Wakinyan (thunder) the giver of rain and reviver of all living things held a revered place in the life of the native. Once a person completed the rites of thunder dreaming, he was accorded special privileges and treated with deference befitting that of a chieftain. His every whim and even his not so pleasant habits were regarded as manifestations of an exceptional mind. As a rule, Indian people held their medicine men in deep respect, regarding them as genuinely gifted people who were able to delve into the secrets of nature. They were accepted and respected without question. At no time could they be subjected to annoyance. Dogs were shooed away; children were kept at a distance; and older people talked in subdued voices. Thunder dreamers possessed mystic powers to alter the course of a severe storm or cause it to disintegrate, so that fresh meat drying in the sun or berries spread out for curing would not be spoiled. So it was said, and so it was believed.

Holy men of ancient times, like modern doctors, performed their beneficent acts for a fee. Gifts of value were proffered before they performed. Their services were in demand in cases such as illness, forecasting, weather predicting and the revealing of personal fortunes.

There is evidence in this portion of the Black Hills indicating that at one time these lush valleys may have been the cradle of an old civilization. Those people of the past were known as *Wita Paha Tu* (dwellers of the Island Hill). Ancient Lakota stories hint that, at one time, the Black Hills were surrounded by a sea. Other legends say the Black Hills were like an oasis, a green, fertile spot surrounded by dry, sun-parched plains, giving the Hills the appearance of a dark island in the midst of a shimmering, mirage-like sea of reflected sunlight. Where these legends came from and what prompted them remains a mystery.

The Lakota of today have been quite aware of the strange footprints of ancient man. *Owe Hanpi,* meaning "their tracks remain" expresses it well in the Lakota tongue. Ancient campsites, the drawings on rock walls, flint quarries whence came the spearheads, arrowheads, stone axes and broken earthenware indicate their long-forgotten presence. They know that ancient peoples once roamed these regions, but they cannot say who those people were, or when and why they disappeared. Only the words *Wita Paha Tu* (dwellers of the Island Hill) vaguely describing the ancients, exist in memory.

The Lakota of today view these evidences of their ancient culture with reverence, saying the relics are the handiwork of a super race which thrived here ages ago, their spirits manifesting themselves only in dreams and in special incidents.

The Indians of long ago also worshipped the awesome

Wakan Gli (lightning) from atop the Thunderhead Mountains because, in the ancient past, on the rolling hills west of those gray rocks, thunder gods slaughtered many buffalo in a drama that stunned mortal witnesses.

Long ago in early summer, the tale begins, a large band of Lakota journeyed into the Black Hills to harvest the many kinds of berries so plentiful in the summer. In those days, multitudes of buffalo and other game animals literally darkened the hillsides with their countless numbers. The buffalo had shed their shaggy winter hair and the fresh grasses made them fat, sleek, and almost black in color.

And so, the story goes, a party of young braves, buoyant and eager, decided on an early morning hunt to bring in supplies of fresh meat. They trotted toward the grazing herds at the break of dawn. A blazing sun rose hotly out of the eastern horizon. Avoiding the heat of the sun, the well-armed hunters moved cautiously along the cool, shady ravines until they came within arrow distance of a small herd of buffalo lazily grazing on the lush grasses. Their plan of action was *Wape Kute,* (ambush shooting).

The young hunters took note of the heavy air. The sun was now higher and beating down more fiercely. Becoming aware of the hot sun and the prospect of rain, which would not be good for the meat if they made an early kill, they agreed to wait out the hot day in the shade of the pine trees.

As they lolled about, or dozed on cushions of dead pine needles, an ominous calm descended. Overhead, thick cumulus clouds boiled and expanded, some hanging menacingly low. The hunters were brave men, ordinarily indifferent to common dangers. But somehow, watching the swiftly changing scene, they became apprehensive. Something sinister was in the air, they felt.

As the swiftly forming storm approached, a windrow of greenish cloud rolled and swirled dangerously low. The hunters thought: "Will the giant turtle let its tail down?" (Lakota say a tornado occurs when a giant turtle in the sky lowers its tail till it touches the ground.) Before any rain fell, however, lightning, like tree roots, flashed grotesquely, striking many objects at once. Thunder claps, reverberating through the craggy hills, shook the ground. The buffalo tossed their shaggy heads as static electrons gathered on the tips of their horns, causing flames like lighted candles to appear.

Disturbed by the heavily charged air, the buffalo swarmed nervously in a tight herd ready for flight before the impending storm. But, before the herd could dash away in a wild stampede, many grotesquely painted giants appeared, mounted on huge white horses. Now there occurred a blinding downpour, as the phantom riders, long spears poised high, came charging down upon the hapless beasts. The giant horses were agile and swift, and they came upon the snorting herd in an instant. Horns clashing, hooves rattling, the buffalo attempted to dodge the hunters of the sky. But with every stroke, a frightened animal toppled like a bolt of lightning. A vicious wind twisted trees apart, hurtling the branches into the air. The awful scene was terrible to behold. A heavy downpour plunged the landscape into darkness. The earth hunters watched in horror as the hellish drama of wanton slaughter unfolded before their unbelieving eyes.

As swiftly as it had come, the storm passed on to the east, leaving calm and sunshine. In the light of the sun there was a shocking scene, with carcasses of dead buffalo strewn over the landscape, their bodies mangled and twisted. Some of the buffalo were already bloating in the hot sun. In the soft, rain-soaked turf the hoof prints of the giant horses cut deep into the spongy soil. It was a spectacle comparable only to a bad dream, as the Lakota are wont to say.

Thus the party of young hunters, in a state of extreme disturbance, returned empty handed to their village, bearing only a lurid tale. The wise men expressed concern. The medicine men interpreted the appearance of the giant hunters as an omen that the god of thunder was displeased. *Waunyan* were offered at once to appease his wrath.

Thereafter those gray rocks (now known as Thunderhead Mountains) were reserved as the hunting grounds of the mighty thunder. Ancient native peoples came here periodically to pay homage and to pray for needed rain.

Devil's Tower

TO THE NORTH AND WEST OF THE BLACK HILLS of South Dakota, there stands another unique natural land formation, rising high into the air. Known as Devil's Tower, it was a renowned landmark and served travelers well. Those who braved these virgin lands relied on this slim tower to get their bearing. It was a dependable sentinel, always a welcome sight.

Devil's Tower and Bear Butte, situated east of the Black Hills, have much in common. Similar in shape, in appearance like pouting children, both stand forever aloof from their parent, the Black Hills. Like Bear Butte, Devil's Tower was a hallowed spire beckoning the native peoples to perform their religious rituals around its base.

This tower was known to the Lakota as *Mato Tipilia* (home of the bears), so named because long ago, many hungry bears met death here when they attacked a group of little Lakota girls. This bear story has always been a favorite legend, delighting Indian children because the little girls were not devoured by the hungry bears as one might have expected, but were saved by Fallen Star, a divine being who graces many Lakota legends.

Scientists who study the earth's formations call these strange towers *laccoliths*, a concentration of hardened lava which forms below the crust of the earth and then worms its way to the surface, much like a grub working its way out from underneath the

65

hide of an animal.

By a merciful act, Taku Wakan caused this sharp mound to rise from the ground in order to save little Lakota children. To this day it stands unchanged, a sacred spire, reminding all Indians that Taku Wakan is kind and merciful.

The Teton Lakota were great travelers, their journeys covering much of North America. They knew the location of salt deposits. They knew where to find pigments for their paints. They made journeys to the northern woods to gather the sweet juices of the maple tree. They lived by the hunt, so they followed the grazing herds of buffalo, and from early springtime to autumn they gathered fruit and edible vegetation.

Thus, it is told, one time a caravan of Teton Lakota was slowly moving toward the Black Hills to harvest the many varieties of fruit abounding there. Such journeys were always leisurely, well-ordered and pleasurable. Everyone, young and old, was in an anticipatory mood. The excitement of new country, new experiences, and the prospect of what lay beyond yonder hill held a thrill of expectation for all. The vanguard scouts went far ahead. Their task was to blaze a trail for the others to travel, while also scouting for water facilities, hunting prospects, natural protective fortifications, and good camping sites.

The flanking scouts moved up and down each side of the moving caravan, keeping a sharp eye for possible enemy movements, watching also for animals to supply fresh meat for the caravan. Within this cordon of alert scouts the marchers were safe from surprise attack. The leaders of the march kept the long column informed of travel orders by heralds who shuttled back and forth as the caravan moved along. Dignitaries, pack carriers, and the *Petilegha Yuha* (carriers of the perpetual fire), brought up the rear. The sick and weak rode on travois.

Socializing was a pleasurable aspect of the march. Matrons moved in groups and exchanged news while caring for the children. New babies arrived without trouble as the caravan moved along. Braves not assigned to duty paired off with young maids. Youths hunted; young children romped and played as they moved along.

When the sun was directly overhead, the caravan halted. All along the column there were hurried preparations for the noon meal. The leaders sat in council and studied the reports of the scouts. Accordingly, further orders were heralded all along the line.

After many days of marching, the Lakota caravan encountered rugged terrain. To the southeast the Black Hills appeared, hazily black. Bears were numerous in the rough piney hills, but as they rarely attacked human beings unless wounded, sick, or hungry, no one feared them.

Then one day, as the travelers moved cautiously through the rough pine-studded hills, an alarm was hastily relayed through the column. Several little girls had wandered off and now were presumed to be lost. Search parties were hurriedly formed and dispatched in all directions. Finally the little girls were spotted, but alas, they were surrounded by a pack of hungry bears. The frightened children screamed for help. No one was near enough to save them. The rescuers, still too far away, looked on in horror as the growling bears closed in on the girls.

Suddenly a voice from the blue sky spoke to the little girls, saying *Paha akili* (climb the hill). It had a strange effect on the attacking bears. For a time they stood paralyzed, giving the little girls a chance to clamber up a small knoll.

The girls huddled together on the hill and hid their faces from the angry bears, as once again the animals, recovering from their surprise, began climbing after them. The situation appeared hopeless, but like the wrath of thunder, the earth shook and groaned as the little knoll, commanded by the strange voice, began to rise out of the ground, carrying the children high into the air. Higher and higher the mound rose, as the frustrated bears growled and clawed at its sides. Sharp pieces of rock broke away from the rising spire and crashed down upon the angry bears.

The children were now safe from the snarling bears, but other dangers loomed. How were they to get down? Appearing like tiny specks on top of a high, sharp mound, they kept their eyes tightly closed, not daring to look down. But the strange voice spoke again, saying, "Do not cry; you will not fall. I have many pretty birds with me. Make friends with them, for soon you will ride upon a pretty bird, away and away down to the ground." And so it was. A covey of birds appeared. The kindly voice belonged to none other than Fallen Star. Molten rocks poured down the sides of the mound, burying the hungry bears. Each little girl now chose a pretty bird upon whose back she flew into the anxious arms of her frantic mother.

That was how Devil's Tower came to be, say Lakota legends. To prove it, the Indians point to the deep crevices along the walls of the tower and the claw marks made by the huge bears of long ago.

Indeed it was so, the Lakota say.

The Sun Dance and Devil's Tower

Devil's Tower has other legends. Those Lakota tribes that traveled the northern plains called the sharp mound *Wiwayang Wachipi Paha* (sundance mounds), because a young man once descended from the Tower, bearing a message from Taku Wakan, commanding the Lakota to perform a prayer dance called: *Wiwayang Wachi,* (gaze at the sun while dancing). Severe and exacting in its rituals, the Sun Dance had strict rules, required painful procedures, and was a test of faith and endurance.

There is no truly accurate written description of the Sun Dance. Perhaps early day writers had no opportunity to witness one as originally performed. Or, they viewed it as a mode of paganistic worship not worthy of space or time, a ritual to be forbidden and shunned, as once it was by the white men, particularly in the latter part of the nineteenth and early twentieth century. A more recent presentation of the dance had been performed chiefly for tourist consumption. It was at best a poor copy of the original. Furthermore, the participants were poorly informed, omitting many significant gestures which have subtle religious meanings. Today, there is a renaissance of the ritual, and hope has been renewed among the Lakota that revival of this observance will mean a revival of the people's cultural values.

The origin of the Sun Dance is lost in antiquity. As originally practiced, the observance took four days and four nights to complete. It had to be held in the heat of summertime, "when the tail of the spear grass curls and the weather prophets foresee a stretch of rainless days." So it is said.

Preparation for the Sun Dance consisted of a series of rituals, climaxed in the four-day endurance dance. It is a religious and worshipful event.

Among the preliminaries was the construction of a shaded shrine built by the elite of the young men as chosen by the Board of Elders who directed religious matters. Those selected had to cleanse both body and soul by doing penance in the *Initipi* (steam hut). The shrine or canopy, a network of poles covered with pine boughs, made in circular form to represent the sun, had its entrance facing east, so that the rising sun would bathe the arena with its first rays. In the center of the arena stood the holy pole.

The search for and selection of the pole was a sacred duty, and the honor was bestowed upon a young girl, clean, chaste, in the

68

bloom of young womanhood. Many young maids vied for the coveted honor. They paraded before the judges and the public, while singers extolled their virtues in lyrical incantations. When one was chosen, she was escorted to the woodlands, where she selected a tall, straight, slender tree. Young men, well coached in the rituals, carefully felled the tree and marched out of the woods with it resting on crossbars. At designated stations along the pathway, they laid down the pole for a brief time and performed prayer gestures. Onlookers wishing to do penance laid their offerings on the ground for anyone to claim.

When the carriers approached the entrance to the shrine, heavy drums boomed. Singers burst forth in rhythmic song. Ground-hallowers swarmed into the arena. Dancing abreast in tight formation, they consecrated the ground and smoothed down the grass. This brief mass performance was called *Owanka Onasto.* The pole was then carried to the center with ceremonial splendor, and adorned with appropriate ornaments. Two large bundles of saplings were tied in the shape of a cross at its tip. In Lakota, this cross is called *Chanwakan,* meaning *holy,* of the spirit, or medicinal.

Legends say one bundle symbolized the invincibility of the Lakota and their many years of unbroken dynasty. The other bundle was placed in homage to Taku Wakan, embodying their laws. Each sapling represented a dictum of their social, moral and spiritual law, and their code of daily living. From the top down, other ornaments were attached in order of their importance. Numerous thongs for the dancers were attached. Before raising the pole, a package of foodstuff was put into the earth-hole in which the pole would lay, to insure economic stability through the winter ahead. Then the pole was raised amid poetic chants and gestures of prayer, all signifying the magnitude and glory of the religious event.

In early dawn ceremonies, the bare-footed dancers (to allow direct contact with mother earth) were called and led to the holy pole with special sacred pipe rituals. Next in order was the act of piercing. The areas of piercing had to be clean and infection free. Medicine men pierced each breast above the nipple making two slits with a sharp knife, then inserting a skewer or thong beneath the skin. Coagulating ointments could be used to avoid excessive bleeding, but the use of pain killers was prohibited. Dancers who wished for added favors would vow to drag a buffalo skull as further penance. In that case their shoulders were also pierced. Other dancers would decorate their bodies with eagle feathers by inserting the stems into the punctured skin.

After the piercing, the dancers were securely tied to the Spirit Pole. They stood facing east. As the red sun appeared over the horizon, the singers, accompanied by the hard staccato beating of drums, burst forth in song, officially proclaiming the ritual dance was now in progress. The dancers, fresh and eager, blew lustily on their eaglebone whistles in rhythm with the drums. Admiring throngs of Lakota cheered.

When the sun finally sank behind the western hills, there was a slight respite from the heat and the brightness of the sun, but with fresh singers the dance went on. Bonfires ablaze, the dancers now limply kept time to the monotonous beat of the drums.

After a day or two, a dancer might attempt to break free by plunging forcefully away from the pole. Friends or relatives would assist him by holding him round the waist. With this added weight, there was a chance that the skin would tear apart. This induced disregard for physical pain was considered heroic by the spectators. There were prolonged ovations of approval. When a dancer fell to the ground from sheer exhaustion, his kinfolk could rush in to help him to his feet, giving him a grape leaf dipped in water to suck upon. If he failed to continue, gifts were offered to anyone who would come forward and free him from further dancing, but the skin had to be cut and not the thong. Every dancer was considered a hero, urged on and cheered by the worshippers.

Thus, much like Bear Butte on the east side of the Black Hills, Devil's Tower held a vital position in the religious practices of the red man.

THE RULES OF LIFE

Standing Bear, Lakota Indian leader, explained the conduct of both children and adults, desirable and encouraged by the Lakota:

"Training began with children who were taught to sit still and enjoy the silence. They were taught to use their organs of smell, to look when there was apparently nothing to see, and to listen when all seemingly was quiet. A child that cannot sit still is a half-developed child.

"Excessive manners were put down as insincere, and the constant talker was considered rude and unthinking. Conversation was never begun all at once, nor in a hurried manner. Only one voice was heard at a time. No one was quick to ask a question, and no one was pressed for an answer. A pause allowing thought was the only courteous way of beginning and conducting a conversation.

"Silence was meaningful with the Lakota. And in the midst of sorrow, sickness, death, or misfortune of any kind, as well as in the presence of the great, silence was the mark of respect. More powerful than words was silence with the Lakota."

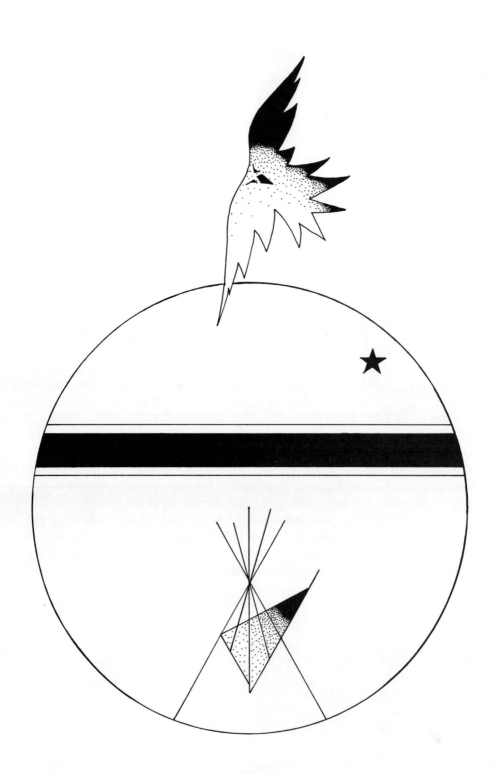

The White Crow

IN THE EARLY DAYS OF SOUTH DAKOTA, Rapid City was a neglected hamlet on the eastern edge of the Black Hills. Today the town is the metropolis of the Black Hills. Deep in a narrow gorge on the east central edge of the hills, the city is impatiently expanding in all directions.

From atop the mountain ridge known as Skyline Drive, one can see a mass of buildings filling up the lowlands of the valley, spreading into the canyons to the west. At night its shimmering lights blaze like a forest in flames.

At one time Hot Springs, Custer, Sturgis, Deadwood and Lead City were the principal towns of the Black Hills. Hot Springs, with its warm waters, boomed as a health resort. Sturgis flourished with the establishment of Fort Meade near Bear Butte. Under the protective eye of the military, gold-hungry adventurers surged over the newly blazed trails; industry followed close behind the advancing hordes. Deadwood, Lead City and Custer were the big boom towns in those hectic days. For a brief time, Rockerville flashed through the sky of fame like a fiery meteor, only to burst in flame and die. Gold mining has been their principal source of growth and renown.

Rapid City, with its water and hay, was then known as the Gateway to the Black Hills. It provided a haven for the migrating gold seekers, as well as the freighters. Rapid City offered a place to lay over temporarily for the caravans of humanity, to water and rest

73

the mules and oxen, wash in the abundant waters, and then move into the Hills.

A fast flowing river known to the Lakota as *Mini Lusa-han Wakpa* (fast water river), runs through Rapid City. Originating somewhere in the heart of the Hills, it tumbles in lively haste over its rocky bed. Due to this perpetual cascade of motion, the river never freezes over, even in the coldest of winters, or so say the Lakota.

The year-round open waters, the profuse growth of deciduous trees, and the high canyon walls made this narrow valley one of the best winter camping grounds for the Indians. Ominous clouds might roll, and cold winds might howl; in the valley there was shelter and calm. Nutritious grasses were abundant, making it an ideal place for buffalo and elk. The Lakota could not have wished for a better natural order of things. Deeply religious, he accepted this unique situation as a personal gift from his God, and paid Him homage in religious rituals.

During one year, ages ago, the icy breath of *Wazia* (keeper of the snows) began to chill the air, and strange things befell the Indian encampment. There was a noticeable absence of game animals, and the winter campers were threatened with scurvy and other diseases.

In those days, the birds of the air and the beasts of the land spoke a common language. Among them, physical power was not the only quality for leadership. Intelligence was an even more admirable quality. Among them all the crow was most respected. The crow at one time was a beautiful bird, graceful, plumey white, possessing a most melodious voice. He was intelligent, a natural leader. Other birds and animals were content to follow him. Thereby hangs the legend of the White Crow. Let us return to the winter encampment of the Lakota, before proceeding with this most unusual story, which has become a legend to be told again and again through the years.

Usually the Lakota expected the winter sojourn to be pleasant, with an abundance of social activities. But this time, as the fall rains turned to winter snows, a shadow of premonition seemed to hover over the village. Buffalo and other game animals were noticeably absent, even though this valley was their favorite winter grazing ground. Hunters had to go far away into distant lands to find fresh supplies of meat. Cold, penetrating winds blew in the swirling snow. The tipis sagged under heavy snow; the whole landscape lay dying under a deep crust of snow. It was risky to venture into the blinding storms; sometimes hunters did not return.

Elders of the *Tipiyokihe* (council lodge) met to deliberate.

Tynweya (watchful eyes, scouts), were sent to investigate the mysterious situation of the animals' absence from their customary feeding grounds. Meantime, buffalo chips were burned in campfires to lure the buffalo with their pungent odor. There were no buffalo nearby to pick up the scent.

One day a scout, who had been gone for many days and was presumed dead, returned bearing a strange tale of a big crow that chased away the buffalo. His story seemed so improbable that he was not taken seriously. A likely story, the people scoffed. "A crow telling buffalo to flee from the hunters!" It was, indeed, difficult to believe, but there were some who thought it might be worthy of a test. Thus, more scouts were sent afield to check the truth of the tale.

After days of searching, the weary scouts came upon a herd of buffalo. Losing no time, they charged the herd. Alas, just as the scout had related, a white crow swooped down out of the frosty sky, yelling at the buffalo to run for their lives. In a screeching voice it said: "You, you shaggy, stupid creatures; you with the flaring nostrils and glassy eyes, run! Flee from these evil beings! They will kill you, drink your blood and eat your flesh. They will use your shaggy hides to keep warm."

The buffalo, heeding these warnings, stampeded. Soon they were out of sight. The crow landed on the back of any buffalo that lagged behind, and with its sharp beak, pecked away until the bison squirmed in pain and joined the galloping herd. The crow soared high, above arrow distance, making sure that the hunters killed no buffalo.

The whole village now felt the pangs of hunger. Many turned gaunt with a wild look in their sunken eyes, their skins dry and dark in the glaring snow. The young children cried out for food. The fish in the river were seined out. Tubers along the river were rooted out and eaten. The inner bark of pine and other trees was peeled and boiled for the pulp and juices. Every known method was used to feed the hungry, but alas, a merciless famine now gripped the village. Howling winds raged overhead; inside the cold and frost covered tipis the young and the weak were dying.

One day the villagers met in mass prayer. They brought tobacco and other *Waunya* (offerings); it was all they had. They sat with heads bowed while the medicine man lighted the prayer pipe. Holding it high, he made all the formal ceremonial gestures; he intoned chants of worship as he pointed to the four principal wind-flows of the earth. He pointed skyward to Taku Wakan, Sire of all living things, then downward to the earth, spawner of all life. He gestured slowly, so that the mystic messengers might savor the soothing smoke of the prayer pipe. "Show us a way to capture or somehow counteract the strategy of the scheming white crow," he intoned.

As the prayer ended, a strange voice was heard, commanding the worshippers to lift their heads and listen: *"Anaghoptan,"* (turn your ears this way), the voice said, "You have hurled your voices to your God to be *Waunshila* (merciful). I am Fallen Star, His *Wahoshi* (messenger). You must not despair, but take comfort in my words, for there is a simple way to subdue the white crow. Outsmart him. First, you must choose two young men. They must be strong, fleet of foot and willing, if need be, to face death. They must disguise themselves as buffalo using hairy robes and a horned buffalo head and, to offset human scent, they must smear their bodies with buffalo manure. Then they must seek out and mingle with a herd. A hunting party must be nearby to give chase."

The appearance of Fallen Star, the divine messenger, brought hope and revived the spirit of the village. People gathered in groups, watching and helping the two volunteers turn themselves into buffaloes. Cleverly they made themselves into shaggy buffaloes, then off they went to join a buffalo herd. Their disguises were clumsy and heavy. The snow was deep, and they were worn and weary when finally they found an unsuspecting herd and moved in. Near the herd, a hunting party lay hidden in the snow, their clothing smeared with white clay to blend with the whiteness of the snow.

Despite all this cover-up, the white crow was not deceived. Before the hunters could charge the herd, the crow had swooped down out of the flaky sky and screeched a warning cry at the herd. "The killers are coming!" The buffalo, alert to the warning, gathered in a tight group and as they sped away in a solid, snorting mass, their horns clacking, one old buffalo lagged behind. The white crow pounced upon the animal pecking away with a beak as sharp as a spearhead. The rear man inside the make-believe buffalo reached out and seized the large, strong crow by its legs. In the savage battle that ensued, it took both men to subdue the screaming, clawing bird.

The young men, severely clawed, shackled the angry crow to a carrying pole with strong thongs, then they returned to the village, carrying the crow with its head hanging down. A bird once so proud was now subdued in shame and disgrace.

Following the instructions of Fallen Star, the crow was brought before the members of the Tribunal. This beautiful white crow, once admired and envied by all, had challenged the superiority of man, causing a famine in which many had died. Now it must pay. The solemn members of the Tribunal decreed that the white crow must suffer lasting disgrace. Its feathers must now be black.

To carry out the decree, the white crow would be tethered to the top of the council lodge at the smoke vent. There it would remain until its white feathers had turned as black as charcoal. "The dead must be avenged," said the elders of the Tribunal. The whole encampment was jubilant, although the march of the mourners was still in progress.

With shouts of triumph, the stronger members of the village grabbed the defiant bird, hoisted it to the top of the council lodge, and securely tied it. A hot fire blazed with pitch pine, so the smoke would be black and sooty.

The white crow, however, was true to its heritage of pride. As the sooty, black smoke clung to its white feathers, it sang bravely in a melodious voice. It sang songs of courage depicting a conquering hero. Then the song changed to lighter, vibrant tales of love. Always with the final notes came the melodious mating call, pleasing to the ear.

The sun rose and set many times, and the days dragged on, as the white crow began to show signs of weariness. The gloss and sheen of its feathers had turned dark and dull. Now the melodious voice was weak and raspy. Its chants were those of a dying warrior. All the while, its snow-white feathers turned darker and ever darker. Then one day, the bird was as black as ripened cherries. Its once envied voice (flutes were made to imitate that voice) was now only a raspy caw.

When the crow was limp and near death, it was taken down, freed of its shackles and allowed to fly away, black, without song; a punishment it must endure for all time. Never again would it oppose man.

Thus, once again Fallen Star, the heavenly being, saved his Lakota people from ultimate tragedy, this time foiling the clever scheming of the white crow.

So they say.

Wind Cave

DEEP IN A NARROW RAVINE IN THE southeastern portion of the Black Hills, there is a little village with all the characteristics of a town, except that its citizens are the caretakers of nationally known Wind Cave. They maintain the facilities for the cave and arrange guided tours for the many people who visit there. The cave and the little town lie hidden in the rolling hills, and a visitor is not aware of them until he is actually descending into the ravine, either from the north or the south.

In history books it is related that a white man, Tom Bingham, discovered the cave in the year 1881, while hunting deer. Wind Cave was designated a national park by an Act of Congress.

However, the Indian discovered this place centuries ago. Places like the wind cave were his landmarks. Some of those landmarks held a deep religious significance for him. Now, those ancient grounds where the Indians lived and worshipped are known by all as places of wonder, for all the world to see.

There are many legends associated with *Washun Niya* (the breathing hole).

This place has been deep in the history of the original American for thousands of years before the advent of the white man. Like many other places in the Black Hills, this "hole that breathes cool air" was a landmark.

Lakota history says that medicine men of ancient times journeyed from far away lands to worship at Washun Niya, and to offer sacrifice. It was their belief that buffalo and other game animals came out of this cave, the animals being bred and supplied by mysterious beings who inhabited the underground regions.

Singers of holy songs came here to capture the soft, sighing sounds that exuded from this great cavity of the earth. Legends say these were the whisperings and the singing of those people who occupy underground lands. The Indian made flutes to imitate the pensive overtones of this hissing hole. Its breath was like a fall breeze. So say the Lakota.

Geological explanations of how the cave was created say that it began long ago, in the early dawn of time. The restlessness of a soggy world: rumbling waters shrouding a young world carrying silt and lime, depositing its cargo here and there only to wash it away at a later era caused the emergence of this natural phenomenon, it is said. The effects of underground rivers, the erosive actions of the elements over a great span of time; these are some of the conditions credited with origins of the cave. Was Wind Cave born in this fashion, long before man? Scientists offer these explanations.

The Lakota do not claim to know how the Wind Cave came to be created. He only relates that it is there, as a link between the upper and the underground world.

Taopi Gli, the son of a Lakota chief, and a *kola* (friend) had always hunted together. On one particular day, breaking away from the main hunting party, they trotted away toward a wooded ravine not too far away.

In late midday they spied a small herd of deer. They stalked their game under cover of trees and shrubbery, until they were within strong arrow distance. The unsuspecting herd lolled and grazed, unaware that soon, one or two would feel the sting of a deadly arrow.

They made their kill and deftly bled their animals. Now they quartered the carcasses, hanging choice cuts here and there on pine boughs to cool in the evening breeze.

As they rested and waited for the meat to cure, the ever-alert Taopi Gli caught a fleeting glimpse of a moving object far down in the shadowy canyon. Ever curious, he arose and noiselessly ambled his way down the steep incline for a closer view of the mysterious apparition. His companion remained on the hill, keeping watch over the curing meat.

As he sat waiting, the day waned, evening shadows now lengthened into ghostly silhouettes, and soon the blackness of night shrouded the landscape. Taopi Gli did not return. The kola, alarmed at the fast deepening dusk, wormed his way down the hill through tangled thickets and over large boulders to search for Taopi Gli.

As he neared the bottom of the hill, behold, there in twilight a romantic scene met his searching eyes. Taopi Gli was seemingly lost in intimate talk with a most bewitching maid. She wore a headband of intricate design, adorned with richly colored plumes of the white-tailed eagle. A creamy buckskin dress draped her young body. As he stared in amazement, the maid, with the instinct of a creature of the woods, furtively glanced about and retreated deeper into the shadows. Taopi Gli followed, as though in a trance. Both finally disappeared in the dark gloom of the canyon. It was a rapturous but an ominous scene.

The kola opened his mouth to shout *Waktayo* (beware), but no words came. He stood helplessly rooted to the ground. Vaguely he remembered the legends of the wicked double-women and what they did to young men.

How long he stood in that frozen trance he did not know, but when he came to his senses it was dark and he was quite alone. He rushed wildly down the ravine. As he came upon the spot where he last saw the lovers, he heard strange hissing noises. With a sharp spear poised for a quick thrust he approached the spot where he had heard the weird sounds. There, on the floor of the narrow canyon, he stumbled onto a small hole emitting a steady flow of cool air. Near the hole were the imprints of the phantom maid's small moccasins alongside the tracks of Taopi Gli. There was silence.

Up and down the narrow canyon he ran, shouting for his friend. There was no response to his frantic calls, only the faint echoes of his own voice came bouncing back to him from the canyon walls. Thoroughly frightened as he imagined what might have happened to Taopi Gli, he ran with a spurt of energy all the way back to the village, remorse nagging at him all the way. He was not certain the beautiful maid was one of those wicked women of old, known as *Winyan Hupapika,* (double woman).

When the fate of Taopi Gli was heralded to the entire village, it was thought he had fallen victim to one such "double woman." Perhaps by now, the people thought, he was in a deep trance, far away, wearily trotting after a phantom woman.

The entire camp was now in mourning for the loss of the young man. But the council elders decreed, that before abandoning all hope, a thorough exploration of the mysterious hole must be made. Many expressed the opinion that Taopi Gli and the strange woman might have been sucked into the "breathing hole."

All the rawhide ropes in the village were collected, then spliced end to end, until there were many long cables.

On a bright day the improvised cables were carried to Washun Niya. The people gathered there, and an appeal was made for volunteers who would dare to crawl into the hissing hole. Many young men, eager for adventure, accepted the challenge. What mysteries lay below that hole with the chilling breath? They would now have a chance to know! The volunteers, with ropes tied to their bodies, descended into the hole amid loud cheering, each carrying a flaming torch and a spear. Again and again they descended. Alas! Each time they returned empty handed. All they saw were grotesque formations and the eerie shadows cast by their flaming torches.

A worthy young man, with promise of a brilliant future, was gone. The baffling mystery of his disappearance only added to the deep grief of the mourners. His parents and friends grieved over his disappearance in a public march of mourning.

As was the custom in those ancient times, the mourners' hair was shorn to a stub, and self-inflicted wounds on the legs oozed blood as they marched along the circular encampment. The young man's personal belongings were strewn on the ground for the needy to pick up. The parents stripped themselves of all their worldly possessions. In their grief, material things no longer held any value.

Knowing that death was inevitable, the Indian judged a man's worth by the way he approached that crossroad and made his exit. His philosophies indicated a fatalistic tendency. He observed that only earth is long-lasting; all else upon it is only temporary. He also observed that death plays an important part in the scheme of life—from the dead leaves that lie fallow, new life springs forth. In all forms of life upon this planet, death is essential that life may continue.

The Indian has always held that unabated mourning is not good for the mind. Thus, a traditional custom known as *Shawichaya,* (to clothe anew) was practiced. This custom is held to this day.

Death is always a shock, and grief is a natural reaction. But people usually recover from their sorrow in time. Some however, do not recover easily. When this happens, the mourners are taken before a special gathering where they are feted and receive gifts. Finally, their mourners' shrouds are taken off in public. With gentle advice to forget their sorrow, they are clothed in new and brighter apparel. A wise man, gifted in the workings of the mind, ministers to them, explaining that prolonged grief is not true sorrow, but a form of self-pity, a sign of weakness. "To counteract your state of mind, a good medicine is to concern yourself with the plight of others," they are told.

Thus, the social orders of the day took turns giving the grieving parents counsel and solace. Nothing helped; the sorrow remained. At last, the medicine men, as a final resort, proposed that the despondent chief seek solace in a special prayer, the *Hanblecheya,* (to seek revelation in a prolonged fast). A fast in the wilderness might soothe the hurt. Perhaps, in a vision, the grieving one would be apprised of the fate of his son.

After the necessary rituals and time spent in the *Initipi* (steam hut), the chief mourner was led away to the mountain to conduct his vision quest. The high peak upon which he must pray was known to the Lakota as *Hechinskayapi Paha,* (spoonhorn or goat mountain). In later years it was renamed Mount Coolidge by the white people.

When the final well-wishes and words of encouragement ended, the escort descended the mountain leaving the chieftain alone upon his quest. He wore no clothing; he had no food or water, and being on a mission of prayer, he had no defensive weapons. To dispel the grip of loneliness, he sang loudly and did the war dance. He prayed and he wept. He did the *Hanbloglaka,* (poetic incantations of heroic incidents in battle). Always, his mind was set upon a single course, to enter into a trance and attain a visual revelation. Or, to receive some message of the actual fate of his son.

After the allotted time of four days and four nights, a party of selected braves was ordered to climb the mountain and bring back the remains of the chieftain. Hanblecheya was one of the most rigorous and austere religious practices of the Lakota. No one held any hope that the chieftain could survive the ordeal.

When the party reached the top of the mountain, they were astounded to find the chieftain very much alive. Though weak from fatigue and exposure, his eyes were alight with new life and knowledge. He told the rescuers that he was now content. He had won a vision.

After an interval of recuperation, the chieftain wished to have an audience with his people. He had a message of great importance for all.

A large fire was set ablaze, warming and lighting up the dark, chilly night for the solemn occasion. Back in the shadows the chieftain stood, a ghostly figure. In solemn, well modulated tones he recounted the events of his rigorous vision quest. For three days and three nights he sang, danced, chanted and wept. He was aware that he was growing weaker, and his mind wandered. He felt that he could not endure the cold, thirst and hunger much longer. On the fourth night, he raised his arms heavenward with extreme effort, in a final gesture of supplication. Then, a strange stupor seized him. He felt free. Weariness and hunger, mental and physical torture, all faded away; he stood calm and strong on top of that lonely mountain. Suddenly he was no longer alone. There appeared before him a man standing upon a luminous bank of fog. The Chieftain knew the strange apparition was that of Fallen Star, the heavenly one who was the son of a Lakota maid. Then there floated before him a series of dream-like scenes, in which he became aware that his son, Taopi Gli, was alive and now a member of the *Maka mahe oyate,* (peoples of the underground regions). There occurred before his very eyes a reenactment of the romantic episode in which his son had been abducted by the fair maid of the underground world.

As the husband of the maid, Taopi Gli was now a high priest, a ruler with prestige and power. But, he must now and for always remain in those below-ground lands.

The Chieftain assured his people that this strange alliance was a good omen, because the "under-the-ground" people were the keepers and breeders of all game animals. By this union of providence, the surface dwellers would never again be visited by famine. The *Washun Niya* would always be the connecting link between the two worlds.

For ages, according to Lakota legend, since the marriage of a surface man to a distinguished girl of the underground world, famines were unknown, because out of the mouth of the Wind Cave, never-ending hordes of buffalo and other game animals emerged as time went on. If it is difficult to believe that large animals such as the buffalo are able to come out of such a small hole, legend explains that the animals came out like a string of tiny ants, but as they emerged and sucked in the invigorating surface air, in a very little time they expanded into their natural sizes. This was indeed true until the white man came, bringing along new conditions, disturbing ancient religious traditions, and burdening the natural world with entirely foreign ways of living.

To the east from Wind Cave there is another landmark of the Lakota, known to the white man as Buffalo Gap. Lakota legends say, that at one time, there was no such gap there. But, through the ages, as countless herds of hungry and thirsty animals came out of the Wind Cave, they would make a wild dash to the eastward to get to the cool waters and lush grasses. Legends say, that after countless years the sharp hooves of the stampeding herds have cut down a high ridge into a narrow gorge. Thus it has become known as the *Pte Tatiopa,* (doorway of the buffalo).

In certain ceremonies, the following song is sung by a holy man of the tribe.

AN ELDER'S SONG

They are sending a voice to me.
From the place where the sun goes down.
Our Grandfather is sending a voice to me,
From where the sun goes down.
They are talking to me as they come.

Our Grandfather's voice is calling to me,
That winged One there where the Giant lives,
Is sending a voice to me. He is calling me.
Our Gandfather is calling me.

ħarney Peak

THE CHOKATA WAS THE EXPRESSION the Lakota used to designate the center of the Black Hills. In this area there are many unique geological formations: the Needles, Mount Rushmore, and Sylvan Lake, to name but a few. But one of the most magnificent features in the Black Hills is Harney Peak, the highest mountain east of the Rockies.

The geological origins of these sharp granite protrudings date perhaps to the infant days of the Black Hills. Some scientists say it was at first only a dome-like bulge. The elements of nature, in a time period so distant that it baffles the imagination, carved away at the bulge, tearing and washing away the soft material, leaving only hard, sharp granite needles pointing skyward.

From the surface of the earth downward, layers of strata, composed of geologic materials, form the crust of the earth. Far down in this laminated formation is a layer of stratum known as granite. Mount Rushmore, Mount Harney, and the Needles are out-croppings of this granite layer. Powerful forces of nature broke up the earth's crust, forcing the granite stratum to the surface.

The Lakota have, at one time or another in their long history, scaled those craggy rocks with the use of long ropes braided from buffalo hide thongs. At one time, so legend says, Lakota braves made a mass assault on Mount Harney in a futile attempt to capture a vulture that lived on top of the mountain.

Hinhan Kagha Paha (Evil Spirit Hill) was the Lakota name for Harney Peak, so called because long ago the most hideous and cruel of all phantom creatures was said to live on top of the mountain. The evil creature was rarely seen, but those who had seen it said it resembled a huge night owl with ugly, yellow eyes. It had large, basket-like ears and flew with the speed of a bat. The monster craved only the taste of young animals and little children. In the darkness of night, it would pounce on young animals or snatch little children out of tipis, throw them into its big ears and carry them back to its lair on top of Mount Harney. There, in a cruel and leisurely manner, it would torment the victims until they died. Then they would be devoured by the monster.

And so, in ancient times, when passing through this rugged terrain, babies and small children were hidden until the caravan was at a safe distance from the mountains and the dreaded creature of Harney Peak.

To tell the story of Harney Peak, let us take a small "stop-over" and find out how the Lakotas lived.

That branch of the Lakota known as the Tetons were a traveling people. In moving from place to place they carried only the barest of necessities. A few household furnishings, some necessary personal belongings and perhaps a few things of value, were all they carried. The man, hunter and warrior, had his weapons upon his person at all times. The woman was in charge of knives and hatchets, although most of her duties consisted of domestic householding and the care of the young. Kitchen utensils were comprised of wooden dishes, spoons and cups made from the horns and hooves of various animals. Wearing apparel, such as extra moccasins, robes and clothing were transported on travois or pack animals.

The Indian walks in advance of his woman, a habit which persists to this day. It is instinctive; the male is ever the protector, clearing the trail while the family follows at a safe distance.

In his travels the Lakota might go a fair distance in one day. Or he might tarry, depending on the abundance of fruit or game. This was his life. He was in no hurry. As the sun sank over the western horizon, wherever he might be, he stopped, and immediately made shelter for his family. Sharpened willow saplings were struck in the ground in a circular fashion, the tops bent towards the center and interwoven into a dome-like framework about four or five feet high. The framework was then covered with matted grass, bark, brush, or whatever else was handy as cover. These huts were easily made and provided livable quarters for the night. In the morning, when he moved on, he simply abandoned the hut. His life habits were such that he was at all times prepared for emergency. If the occasion arose, he could move with the swiftness of the wind.

The Teton Lakota had other types of dwellings, one was the cone-shaped tipi of slender spruce poles covered with tanned buffalo hides sewn together. This type of dwelling was called *Tushu Tipi,* (lodge pole house.) Although they could be set up or dismantled in short order, the long poles and the hide covering made a bulky and cumbersome load for moving. They were not particularly convenient for traveling, but were excellent for winter camping. An opening at the top served as chimney and air vent. Two flaps at the top, operated from the ground by regulating poles, controlled the draft and tipi temperature.

When a stay of longer duration was planned, rocks were placed around the bottom of the tipi, stabilizing it against strong winds, as well as to keep out the winter frost and prowling night rodents. Some of these tipis are preserved to this day as tokens of a happier era.

The cutting of lodge poles was a community affair during springtime when the bark was loose from the trunk and could be stripped off more easily. The canyons, reaching down from the top of Mount Harney, the Needles, and the dark canyons of Spearfish Creek, were favorite cutting grounds for such poles. The Lakota made their spring pilgrimages into the heart of the Hills, always with exuberance and happiness. The cutting and curing of lodge poles was an art, and some men knew their profession well. If a pole warped, water and a little oil were applied at the right places. By rotating it in the sun, one could achieve a fine straight pole. The poles were measured and sorted into their proper lengths and sizes. The *Akatinpi* (extended arm) was generally accepted as a standard of measurement.

The size of a man's tipi was a good measure of his prominence in a band. Chieftains and men of affluence lived in large tipis, and the number of *Ohiye,* (measure of width) lent added prestige. The influential Indian also painted his deeds and accomplishments, as well as his membership in the respected Societies, on the outside of his tipi, using symbol language.

Once upon a time, so the legend says, many bands of Lakota moved into the heart of the Black Hills to cut lodge poles. After the busy working activities of the day, there were social affairs in the evenings. There were games, contests and dancing for the young. The elderly smoked their pipes, discussed the day's events, and made plans for the coming day. Contentment held sway, or so it seemed.

Nearby was that formidable *Hinhan Kagha Paha,* Harney Peak. Despite the apparent gaiety and the social activities, such evenings brought a vague sense of premonition to the encampment. No one was truly at ease or fully relaxed. In the late evenings, when the campfires smoldered and the people slept, strange noises could be heard, much like the swishing sounds made by the flapping wings of a giant bird in flight.

One night, amidst this uncertain atmosphere, a little girl inside the tipi of a young couple was unusually fretful. Her parents did everything to please the unhappy child. They gave her tasty tidbits to eat, her mother improvised playthings for her, sang lullabies and told stories. Nothing helped. At last, in desperation, the young mother led the little girl to the doorway and said half in fun, "Wanaghi le ichu," (ghost, get this naughty child).

As though someone waited for those very words, a huge, scrawny, claw-like hand reached in and snatched the child away from the mother and out of the tipi. The mother fainted. The child's frantic screams reverberated through the narrow canyon walls. The whole village was instantly awake, aware that something dreadful had happened. In near panic, parents concealed their babies and small children as best they could.

Far away in the dark, gloomy night, the faint cries of the terrified child echoed through the deep valleys. Sometimes there would come a brief silence, then the child would cry out again in agony. Legend says the vulture would croon to the little girl and then whip her with the stem of a rosebush, until blood appeared like raindrops.

At last the cries were heard no more. There was sadness and weeping in the lodge.

After this tragic happening, the babies and young children were guarded and hidden. Campfires burned brightly all through the night. Young men took turns standing guard, watchful and ready for any emergency. But alas, despite all precautions, the flying vulture came again the following night and stole another little girl. Every night thereafter a little girl was snatched away, until four had been taken to the same cruel fate as the first victim. The children cried in terror and pain, but neither the parents nor the warrior guards were able to help them.

Finally the braves decided to make a mass assault on Mount Harney, in an attempt to capture the vulture and rescue the children. They set out with weapons and scaled the craggy cliffs with long ropes braided from buffalo hide thongs. They made a thorough search of the mountain. The children could not be found. All attempts were of no avail. The creature was extremely elusive. And so the braves finally returned to the encampment.

The people were stunned. All bowed their heads in mourning. The parents of the stolen children prayed to Taku Wakan to help them avenge their terrible loss. *Waunyan* (sacrificials) were offered, in the fervent hope that God might reveal a way to combat the vulture before it carried away any more children. There was talk of leaving the encampment and fleeing the hills that sustained such a vicious curse. Already many were busy taking down their tipis and making preparations for a hasty flight. The despondent parents gathered on a hilltop for one last prayer. As they sat with bowed heads, a man in the simple garb of a Lakota warrior appeared before them.

The saddened people knew somehow that this man was none other than Fallen Star, the divine helper of the Lakota people. He eased their sorrow with comforting words, saying that the evil monster, that stole their children and carried them away in its big ears, would never again torture little children because he, Fallen Star, had slain the cruel monster.

He then told the grieving parents to look westward through a mountain. The mountain suddenly became transparent. There, in a vision, they once again saw their children. The little girls stood perched atop the highest pinnacle, on the mountain now known as Needles. Joyous smiles played upon their faces.

Looking into the yearning faces of the parents, Fallen Star explained that certain transitory conditions had already taken place and the little girls would never again be happy among earth people. He comforted them, saying, "Do not grieve. I, Fallen Star, will always be their guardian father."

To the Indian the stars were the handiwork of Taku Wakan. The Lakota say, "In the skies there are places for the *Maghpia Oyate* (cloud people), who were far superior in every way to *Wichasha Akantu* (earth people).

Sometimes, on a cold winter night, when you are alone and far away from the din and glare of the city, look heavenward to the star-studded sky. The Milky Way, like a shimmering mass of fireflies, stretches across that endless dome. Somewhere near this

91

luminous trail you may see a group of little stars, huddled together (Pleiades, daughters of Atlas), faintly twinkling as though talking in whispers. The Lakota say these stars, grouped so closely together, are the little girls whom Fallen Star once rescued from the phantom creature of Hinhan Kagha Paha, Harney Peak.

And so the legend ends.

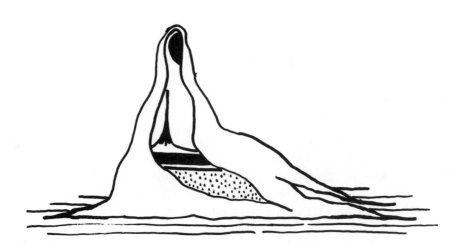

Iktomi

EVERY INDIAN TRIBE HAS ITS OWN STORIES. Some are serious historical narratives. Others are bedtime stories for children, usually carrying a moral. Still others are "fun" tales strictly for sophisticated adult entertainment. The Lakota called these fable-like narrations Iktomi Legends, tales of human frailties, for in them one may find a message.

Stories about an individual known as Iktomi are numerous, providing fun, telling a serious tale, or supplying a moral judgment. Iktomi was an imaginary person. Generally he is described as a quick-witted schemer with a glib tongue. A prankster and a satirist was he, always ready with a sharp phrase. He was eager to shatter favorite dogmas, to prick the sensitivities of the vain. He scorched the pompous of their self-aggrandizement, and he had no regard for moral values.

In these Lakota fables Iktomi played various roles, portraying the foibles common to mankind. These simple parables were narrated in a light and amusing fashion. The listener could piece together the moral as he was able, or as he pleased.

People the world over know the fables of Aesop, the legendry of the Bible, and the moralities of such religious systems as Buddhism. But little is known of the rich folk legendry of the Indian. Part of this wealth of literature is made up of the tales about Iktomi.

93

Contrary to the notions of many people, the Indian was a moralist. Without a Bible or stone tablets to guide him, having no written alphabet, nor written laws to guide him, he lived a truly moral life. He lived, if the truth were known, by the white man's professed moral standards. He had unshakable moral precepts, telling amusing tales to illustrate what happens when one fails to heed the edicts and customs of social living. Such were the tales of Iktomi.

Now we let the Teller of Tales give his listeners these fables of Iktomi the trickster.

Iktomi and his Bag of Songs

ONCE UPON A LONG TIME AGO THERE LIVED one known as Iktomi, whose home was in a small village. He was not a good citizen, and the villagers were not proud of him. He showed no interest in civic affairs; he viewed with distaste such necessary functions as the hunt, warfare, and other matters of public concern. Though lazy and shiftless, his life was an easy one. He lived off the gullibilities of his fellow men. There came a day however, when his bag of tricks soured and back-fired. He became a man despised, without friends. This was a bad time for Iktomi, but he was not worried. He thought it was about time anyway to look around, see new faces and find fresher fields in which to ply his trade.

It was customary, in ancient times, that when a person of note was setting out on a long journey, he was feted and given gifts of moccasins and concentrated foods for his journey. Iktomi had no friends, so there were no farewell parties nor gifts, and no final friendly handshakes.

He was soon on his way with his meager belongings heading northward to new adventures. After a few days of uneventful marching he realized that he must quickly find something to eat. The hurt in his belly was causing his mind to wander. He felt sick. As the hot sun bore down upon him, his pace slowed. He was famished.

Now in a state of despair, he came to the rim of a high ridge. Behold! There before him was a wide valley, with a heavily wooded stream, cutting green, rounded patterns as it wound its way down the beautiful valley, finally disappearing far away in a hazy mist. Dizzy with hunger and fatigue, Iktomi was uncertain. Was this the dream of a starving man? He shook himself and squinted, but there it was, no wandering of the mind, no mirage! Though weak and wobbly, he ran down the hill as fast as his legs could carry him, threw himself down at the edge of the stream, and plunged his head into the cool water. He moistened his dry throat, and sipped a little water at intervals until he felt fully revived.

He must find something to eat, he told himself. He arose and stumbled along the edge of the stream. There before him, in a widened eddy, a flock of ducks were floating around, contentedly riding the small ripples. He was so hungry he was about to dive in, grab a few and eat them alive. But wait! There must be a better way, he decided.

An idea flashed through his mind. Sneaking back into the thickets, he began stuffing a bag with grass as fast as he could. When the bag was full, he threw it over his shoulder and nonchalantly walked along the edge of the stream where the ducks could see him. The ducks saw Iktomi with the big bag. Why the big bag, they wondered?

The curious ducks called to Iktomi, but he pretended not to hear them. He was not about to go out of sight, however. The ducks, unable to restrain themselves, started up a quacking clamor, begging Iktomi to tell them what he had in the big bag and why he must hurry on. With a grand display of impatience he stopped, and grudgingly told the ducks to mind their own affairs and not delay him with trifles as he must hurry on to the next village. "Why, why?" The ducks quacked. "Because," Iktomi said, "There is going to be a grand festival and I am the chosen singer for their dances. These are my songs." He tapped the bag and made as though he was about to hurry on, when there was an outburst of more quacking. "Please stay, we want to dance. Sing a nice song for us and we will dance." Iktomi pretended to be annoyed. He fumed and fussed. At last he agreed to sing for them. "This song is strictly for ceremonial dancing, so be careful and obey its commands. It is called the 'shut eye' song, which means you must dance with your eyes tightly closed. You will have red eyes if you open them before I finish singing," he said. The little ducks, so eager to dance, nodded their heads as Iktomi sang:

"Ishto gomus wachi po   "With eyes tightly closed,
  Ishto gomus wachi po   ye must dance

96

Tuwa yatunwanpi kin
Ishta nisha sha kte."

With eyes tightly closed,
ye must dance
To you who dare to see
Forever red thine eyes
will be."

The dumply little ducks came out of the water and wad-
dled around in rhythm with the beat, their eyes tightly shut. Iktomi
did not miss a beat in his singing as he knocked the fattest ones over
with a stick. One little duck, not so trusting, opened its eyes and saw
what Iktomi was doing. "Open your eyes, you fools, Iktomi is killing
you," said the duck. The ducks who remained alive flew away in a
flash. Iktomi was elated. His scheme had worked well. He had
enough ducks for a few day's supply.

Iktomi had no further use for his bag of songs, so he
dumped the grass out, gathered up his ducks, and put them in the
bag. Next, he mused, he needed a quiet place to roast the ducks.
Trees being plentiful, he selected a spot, built a fire of ash wood, and
when there remained plenty of hot embers, he buried the ducks
under the hot coals for a barbecue.

With the savory scent of roasting ducks pleasantly teas-
ing the appetite, Iktomi thought a short nap was in order before the
big feast. He tried to sleep, but couldn't. A gusty wind was blowing.
High up in the treetop, two large branches rubbing against each
other made harsh, squeaky sounds. Iktomi, a juicy meal awaiting
him, was in an expansive mood. He called up to the branches:
"Brothers, do not quarrel. You are of the same blood. Do not use loud
words." While trying to appease the feuding brothers, the wind blew
harder, making the racket much worse. Iktomi, to prove his noble
intentions, climbed up the tree, and as a gust of wind blew the
branches apart, he stuck his peace-making hand between the quar-
reling branches. You guessed it. There was a sudden lull. Iktomi was
helplessly stuck way up there in the tree top, a hand wedged between
two large branches. The aroma of roasting ducks floated up and
gently caressed his nostrils.

While perched on high, Iktomi had a panoramic view of
the countryside. He could see a fox trotting here and there far away,
as though following a scent. His nose close to the ground, the fox
would run, then stop, lift up his head and sniff the air. Iktomi could
see that the fox looked awfully gaunt. Perhaps he hadn't had anything to eat in days.

Finally, the hungry fox gave up and was about to trot
away when Iktomi, no longer able to contain himself, shouted at the
departing fox: "You scavenger, don't you dare come near here. I have

some nice, fat ducks roasting in the ashes and I don't want any moocher sneaking around here expecting a hand-out!"

The fox stopped, sniffed the air, and said, "Ah, so it is true, my nose never deceives me." Despite a scream-tirade from Iktomi, the fox now followed the scent straight to the smoldering fire. The fire had died down; the ducks lay in the ashes. The fox snatched out a juicy duck, tore the tender, steaming meat from limb to limb, savoring every morsel, while Iktomi drooled and slobbered with rage and hunger.

In spite of Iktomi's nasty temper, the fox was in a jovial mood. He invited Iktomi, between bites, to climb down and join him in the sumptuous banquet of roast duck.

"I would gladly bring a duck or two up to you, but unfortunately I never learned to climb a tree, so hurry and get down here before the ducks get cold," he said. Iktomi could hear the crunching noises as the fox chewed away on the delicate, tasty bones.

As food found its way into the empty cavities of his belly, the fox grew relaxed and more kindly. After all, he mused, the ducks belonged to Iktomi. He should at least leave one or two for him; even diplomats have to eat now and then. The kindly fox called up to Iktomi and told him of his humane plans.

He really wanted to carry out his good intentions, but his appetite was still in fine shape. There was room in his stomach, and the ducks tasted so good he kept eating away. Finishing one duck, he decided to eat just one more, and leave the others for Iktomi. He raked over the coals. Alas, to his dismay, no more ducks. "What a thoughtless glutton I am! Oh well, Iktomi will understand. He is a man of noble tendencies. Right now he is on a peace-making mission, and perhaps not at all hungry," said the fox to himself.

Duck banquets were not an everyday affair for the fox, and so, with a full stomach, he felt the urge for a nap. Yawning, he stretched out right there on Iktomi's grass cushion and slept like an innocent babe. He awakened fully refreshed, in the best of spirits. Before taking his leave, like a true gentleman, he thanked Iktomi profusely for the festive meal. Next time, said Mr. Fox, when Iktomi again had roast duck, he must not forget his old friend, the fox. With those gracious parting words the fox trotted away.

When the fox was just a dot in the shimmering rising heat waves, a gust of wind blew the branches apart. Iktomi jerked his numb hand away and climbed down. He ranted and tore at his straggly hair, screaming insults at the fox and the world in general. All that was left of the ducks was a stale odor and a few bones.

In this Iktomi story one may find a few lessons. The world is full of confidence men, each having his own brand of shut-eye songs. We all have the habit of opening our mouths at the wrong time. And, it would be nice if we could learn never to mess around in other people's affairs.

So goes the story.

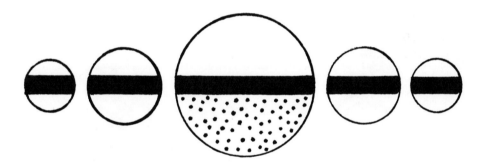

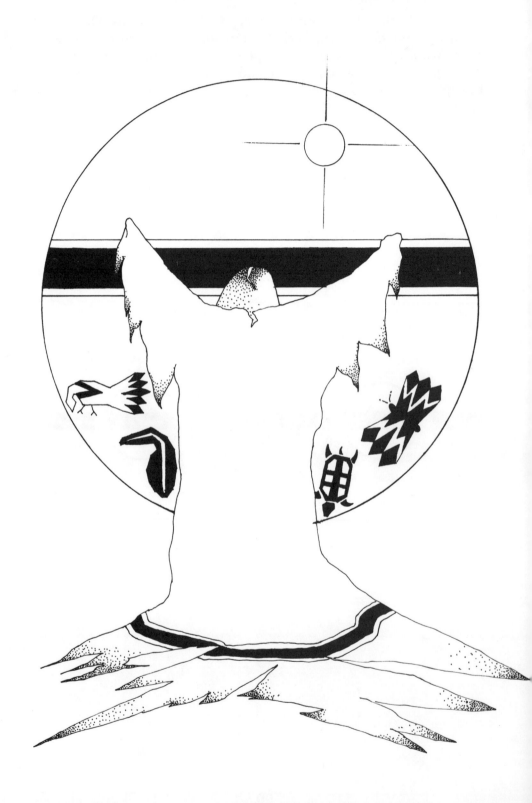

Iktomi the War Hero

IKTOMI WAS NOT A BRAVE MAN. He despised and feared war. A blurred mind, body weariness, futility, and humiliation did not appeal to Iktomi. However, he was also a compulsive braggart.

Many years ago a group of young men, eager and impetuous, decided to taunt fate by entering enemy lands. Their aim was to loot, returning home with prized trophies and some ponies. As the young braves hurriedly gathered their war gear for the long march, someone jokingly dared Iktomi to join the war party. He accepted the challenge with much bravado. The young warriors, unhappy with the result of their jest, then tried to dissuade Iktomi from his rash decision. He was adamant; he even boasted what feats he would perform in the heat of battle.

After many days and nights, and by diligent scouting, the war party knew they were in enemy lands. An encampment of many lodges was not far away. Hurriedly they reviewed their battle plans. With blood curdling war whoops, they would rush in at dawn, throw the sleeping village into a state of panic, and in the mad confusion, gather up the best ponies and make their getaway.

But, as they approached the village, they found a most formidable foe awaiting them. Hopelessly outnumbered, the Lakota made a hurried retreat, but the enemy, astride fresh ponies, easily gained ground. Soon an occasional enemy arrow swished over their heads. The young warriors, eager to make a name for themselves, took turns counter-attacking the charging enemy, giving the slower ones time to gain ground.

After some weary days of dodging the counter-fighting, the young men at last eluded the enemy, leaving some of their comrades behind either dead or captured.

Footsore and gaunt, the survivors returned to their village. Though they had suffered disaster, the villagers accorded them a hero's reception, by making merry and feasting. The heroes were given honored seats in the big reception lodge. In the evenings, as the people cheered, each warrior recounted the heroic role he had played in the now famous retreat. They put a few extra frills into their yarns of bravery lending color and excitement, causing cheers and war whoops from the men, and screech owl calls from the women. After each talk, the war drums boomed approvingly.

Then it was Iktomi's turn to relate his daring exploits in the now glorious battle. In superb oratorical style, he painted a word picture of a dashing warrior singlehandedly holding off the enemy. The uninformed were held spellbound by the rhetoric, but audible boos could also be heard. Someone shouted "Kanghila" (coward like a crow).

In a moment, his fellow braves revealed the true story of Iktomi's claim to bravery. The truth was that while some of the warriors had bravely held the enemy at bay, Iktomi's fear-deadened legs had refused to function. His comrades had to carry him away from the battle. Betrayed, Iktomi bolted for the doorway, pelted with breechclouts, the Lakota way of showing contempt.

The breech-clout treatment humiliated Iktomi. His image as a courageous warrior was shattered. How could he ever brighten his tarnished name and regain his former stature as an upright, fearless young man? Thus he meditated.

Soon thereafter, Iktomi wandered off to spend many moons in self-exile. In solitude he considered the problem of casting off the stigma of cowardice.

Alone in the silent world, the big idea came to him. The solution was simple. First, he must recruit a formidable army. Then he must find and avenge the enemy who caused him to suffer humiliation. Two stupendous tasks, but he could not despair. His reputation was at stake. So he thought, and planned, and pondered.

As he wandered over the desolate land looking for probable soldiers, frustrations were many. Thoroughly discouraged, he was turning homeward, when he met a mud turtle aimlessly crawling. They sat down for a pow-wow. Iktomi at length laid down his plans for a big war. Oddly enough, the turtle showed much interest and advanced the idea that war and fame were brothers. Without further delay they formed an *Olakota kagha* (alliance). The usual vows of allegiance were exchanged with the usual pompous speeches. A few hurrahs for the success of the coming expedition were thrown in for good measure.

The two, much elated, sallied forth in search of more warriors to create an allied force. They met a turkey and again had a war council. Why not, the turkey reasoned. Casting aside a dull life and going to war might be exciting and venturesome, so he too joined Iktomi's army. The next recruit was a butterfly idly bouncing about. Against the glib tongue of Iktomi, he had no chance. Now they were four.

Iktomi was rather proud of his expanding army but he had other worries. His soldiers had no weapons. The bees, snakes and mosquitoes carried their own weapons but Iktomi did not think they were trustworthy. His recruits, anxious to do battle, were already beginning to grumble, when they met a skunk. Iktomi had no trouble persuading the timid, simple-minded creature to join the battle ranks.

To be sure, the recruits looked messy; nevertheless Iktomi was proud of his warriors. But, he reasoned, he must also begin moving his army before discord broke out among the strange assortment of braves. So, soon thereafter, Iktomi in command, a formidable army marched away to invade far off lands, to conquer and to plunder.

The march was tedious, and there was a conflict of personalities. The turkey aimed his nasty temper at the turtle. He was too slow; he had a musty odor. In return, the turtle called the turkey "Mr. Scrawny Neck" or "Mr. Scabby Head." All kept their distance from the skunk. The constant bickering depressed their general, Iktomi, but just as he was about to call off the crusade, they found themselves in hostile country.

Iktomi was not only a bungling general but an unlucky one as well. Early one morning he and his army were roused from their slumber by a band of frightful-looking warriors, with tempers matching their looks. The Iktomi army was captured without a single blow. The odd assortment of General Iktomi's buffoons they had captured did not help improve the enemy's foul tempers. Grumbling loudly, they went into a hurried war conference.

Soon, two fierce looking warriors came and roughly yanked Iktomi to his feet. "Come with us," they said, taking him before the enemy chieftain, who grabbed him by the nape of the neck and shook him. Angrily, he said, "You little weasel, tell me what scares your men. Even the bravest of warriors have their phobias. Tell me their weaknesses and I may spare your life."

Iktomi had a hard time controlling his knees, but with a show of aplomb he went into his pitch, his crafty mind in fine form. "To reveal the innermost secrets of my warriors would be a breech of the most sacred ethics of warfare, a traitorous betrayal committed against my brave warriors, and this is strongly against my conscience and principles. But if you will spare my life, I will break the time-honored code of all high chieftains and reveal to you how each can be tortured into a shameless, whimpering fool." His imagination was now alight, and General Iktomi continued,

"The turkey is a fearless warrior but he cannot stand lofty heights. If you wish to torture him, take him up on a high cliff and push him off.

"The butterfly looks delicate but he is tough and shifty. However, he can't stand the swish of a swift arrow. If you shoot many arrows at him, he will die of fright.

"By nature skunks are docile, timid creatures. They spend their days hiding and come out only at night time. Furthermore, they are so shy, that lifting a skunk's tail, causes him to die of shame.

"As for the turtle, he hates water. He never washes, and the idea of drowning causes him to have cold sweats. If you wish to torment him, ask him if he would like to go swimming in a deep pond." Thus did Iktomi make a shambles of the age-old sacred code of warfare. He revealed the way in which each of his warriors could be subjected to an undignified death.

There was a short time of anxiety as the vicious warriors held another war huddle. With jubilant war whoops, two warriors rushed over and grabbed the hapless turtle by the tail. He was to be the first victim, and it just so happened that a deep pond was near by. His claws cutting deep grooves in the ground, he was dragged to the water's edge. He begged for his life, but was shown no mercy as he was rudely heaved far out into the pond. For a short while, he struggled to keep his head above water. But finally, amid gleeful enemy shouts, the poor turtle sank out of sight.

As the motley crew stood trembling, wondering who would be next, again two warriors marched forward and grabbed the turkey by his scrawny neck. His feeble efforts to resist only angered the warriors. They yanked him along, roughly dragging his limp body toward a high cliff. "Spare my life and I will tell you how Iktomi can be tortured," he begged. His tormentors, grinning sadistically, carried him to the highest pinnacle, and ignoring his pleas for mercy, pushed him off. As the poor turkey fell, the enemy warriors bounced around in a victory stomp. The turkey spread his powerful wings and flew away.

The butterfly was next. He, too begged for a little pity. "I live only to spread joy. Life can be wonderful if all living creatures would stop preying on each other." The enemy had no ears for sermons. At the command of their leader, the warriors covered their bows with arrows and as they shouted, "Howana" (all ready now), many arrows sped after the poor butterfly. Skillfully, he zoomed straight up into the air, and then dove down in the blink of an eye. Right and left he zigged and zagged. Even lightning would have had difficulty following that butterfly's trail. In a short time the bowmen had wasted all their arrows. They watched in astonishment as the butterfly leisurely flew away.

Something was amiss, and the enemy warriors angrily shouted dire threats at the remaining captives as they summoned Iktomi. "You, Two-Face, you lie," they growled. "If something else goes wrong, you will suffer a worse fate than all your braves put together." An angry warrior kicked at the skunk and threatened to kill the timid creature right there on the spot. But they were curious too. They knelt in a circle and began abusing the skunk, making obscene remarks. The gruffest of the lot took hold of the skunk's tail and gave it a yank. With a whirling motion, the skunk squirted its burning venom into every enemy eye. Screaming, they threw themselves on the ground kicking and writhing in pain.

As they lay helplessly blinded and squirming in agony, Iktomi and his motley cohorts rounded up the enemy's fine ponies and galloped victoriously away.

Iktomi made a triumphant return to the village that had humiliated him with the clout treatment. He was now a hero, an honored man with all the appropriate insignias.

The lessons that the Indian saw in this tale of "Iktomi the War Hero" are that obstacles can be surmounted and misfortunes can be dispelled, if one only has the will. The animals remind us that every man, regardless of his station in life, has some redeeming gift that distinguishes him in the eyes of his fellow man.

The Love Life of Iktomi

L ONG, LONG AGO, IN A LAKOTA VILLAGE, there lived an impetuous lad who had all the unsavory earmarks of an *iktomi*. He had precocious ways as a small boy. At puberty he wished to marry. He had no fixed aims; he loathed all the normal ambitions of other boys. Yet, he wanted to marry.

The harassed father sternly lectured the young lad: "Son, you are too young. Your coupstick is still bare of ornaments. No eagle feather has yet graced your hair. Your emotions have yet to awaken. First, you must learn to endure hardships; you must learn the art of restraint, have control of your being. Your arrow must be swift; your arms strong to draw a heavy bow. You must be decorated in public rituals for bravery. When ornaments hang from your coupstick and plumed feathers adorn your brow, it is then proper to enjoy wedded life.

The lecture was wasted. Without hesitation the boy said: "Father, do you remember the legend of the spirit who sang a love song? That spirit now mourns in futile anguish the joys of the living, the pleasures and the happiness of the young. That young man did not have to die! Enthralled by the war drums, he sought fame, he craved public adulation, alas, a temporary glory. In a hysteria of false values, he went away to do battle. Now he lies in dust and bemoans his tragic fate. You yourself have told me it is the philosophy of the Lakota that: While the face is smooth, life is at its best. We must not let it slip by,

106

but must live life to its fullest." (This axiom is comparable to the white man's: 'Gather ye rosebuds while ye may, Old Time is still aflying.')

After a slight pause while the elder pondered these words, Iktomi continued, "Let me have my pleasures now. Later I will do brave deeds and seek public adulation." The father, startled at such mature reasoning, was silent.

Only a few lodges away, Iktomi had already laid low a shy young maid. That evening, after massaging himself with the pungent odor of a lotion made of spruce shavings and oils, and chewing gum of sweet grasses and resin, he made his way to the lodge of his maiden fair. Iktomi had turned fourteen, and his voice was giving him trouble. It had an annoying way of cracking into a falsetto, then descending down to a bass rumble. With this changing of the voice, he began experiencing unexplainable sensations both pleasurable and frightening.

In ancient times women were courted by many men. It was the woman who actually made the choice. Braves who thrilled and quickened the heart-beat were encouraged to return. Iktomi was no warrior: he had still to experience the hunt, and he lacked the suavity of his older competitors. But he had a glib tongue. His romantic chatter brought a glow to the cheeks of this freshly matured girl, and a throbbing sensation to her heart.

Soon thereafter, in free and easy mating rituals and choice words of wisdom, Iktomi assumed the responsibilities of family living. Gifts were strewn on the ground for the needy to pick up, and there was feasting. Festivities over, the young couple retreated to a secluded lodge.

In due time the young couple came out of seclusion, ready to accept the grim realities of ordinary living. They moved in with the girl's mother.

Iktomi's mother-in-law had married early in life. She was left a widow after her first and only child was born. Her man, a warrior bold, had gone away to do battle in far off lands. He had never returned. The widow, a comely woman, was desired and courted by worthy braves, but she had not remarried.

The Indian, like all peoples, had social ethics that guided his behavior in family and social living. Perhaps some of these customs seem absurd today, but along with the wise rules, all were assiduously adhered to.

Constant respectability and formal reserve were expected in brother-sister relationships. In discourse, polite and proper language was the rule. Parent-child relationships allowed for more freedom of emotion, manner, and language. Care and patience from the parent; respect and obedience from the child, were set rules. Father and son-in-law relationships exacted formal cordiality and mutual dignity. All other in-law relationships allowed for considerable freedom in discourse and uninhibited behavior. Ribald joking, snide insults, and pranks were considered proper among in-laws. Taking offense at verbal jibes or practical jokes was thought to be childish, and only brought on further ribbing.

The hard rule was in the son and mother-in-law relationship. Any outward familiarity either way was frowned upon as indiscreet; to face each other or talk to each other was considered brazen. Only in dire emergency must they speak to each other. These old customs are understood to this day.

There wouldn't have been a need for this sordid fable, if Iktomi had been a good citizen. However, the young husband was intensely human. When he first laid eyes on his mother-in-law he took another look and liked what he saw. He decided then that there was no sense in pitching a new lodge of his own. The present plan was ideal.

As time went on, Iktomi was in a turmoil of conflicting emotions. He was well aware of the tribe's strict social ethics and he wanted to abide by them. He did comply with tradition for awhile. But there was his mother-in-law, a ravishing female; the charm of the woman made clear thinking impossible. At nights when he retired he made desperate love to his eager bride to smother those immoral desires he had of his mother-in-law. He was certain a closer relationship with his young bride would, in time, lessen those evil longings. He was wrong. There was no peace. Many a time, in ecstatic embraces with his bride, there was a feeling that it was his mother-in-law he held in his arms. Things were getting out of control.

In the mornings he unconsciously planned his activities so that he would spend plenty of time in the lodge. Sometimes he would tell his wife that he felt ill and must remain in bed, but from under the robes he would keep a furtive eye on his mother-in-law as she went about her daily chores.

In olden times the only bodily covering the Indian had were dressed hides of animals. Tanned buffalo hides sewn together were used for shelter. Certain portions of the buffalo hides were shrunk to make shields and soles of moccasins. Robes were made from hides tanned only on the flesh side of large animals. Deer antelope as well as the smaller animals provided the softer materials for baby and feminine wear. The women wore their dresses short for a good purpose, to insure easy movement. The hem of the dress came just below the knee. Some tribes wore boot style moccasins with wrapping that came above the calves of the legs. Lakota women wore leggings that covered their legs up to the knee, where they were held up with fancy womanly frills. A woman at work might stoop and for an instant reveal a portion of the upper leg. Such an occasional glimpse was always a pleasurable sight to the masculine eye.

Iktomi found great pleasure in watching the uninhibited movements of the mother-in-law. He would study her closely from under the robe. The imagined warmth, the softness, her probable reaction to the touch of male hands took hold of his imagination. It was a little game he played; sometimes his patience was rewarded with a glimpse of a soft-mature leg. There were times when, by sheer effort, he resisted the impulse to jump up and touch her. The strain was exhausting; something must be done.

Iktomi was finally struck with an ingenious idea. It was a daring one and it meant a lot of scheming laced with many lies, but if the scheme should materialize as planned, it would be worth many sacrifices.

In line with his new plan, he took a sudden interest in civic affairs, which kept him seemingly busy elsewhere. His absence from the tipi was a relief to the mother-in-law.

He confided to his wife that he had found his true calling at last. His favorite topic of conversation now was the complexities of government, all of which was meaningless to the young woman. Her main concern was that Iktomi was gone too much of the time, especially at night time, and she said so.

Iktomi explained his absence by saying that he had been deeply involved with the Fox Society and had been attending their meetings regularly. This was hard to believe, because the Fox Society catered only to the young and daring braves, renowned for their courage and valorous deeds. Iktomi insisted he had been an honored guest and was now seriously considering becoming a member of the exclusive brotherhood, because it meant prestige. Who knows, he declared, it might even mean the road to chieftainship! Each evening he mumbled a few excuses and left the lodge. He did not return until just before dawn. The young wife was now positive that Iktomi was seeing another woman. She sniffed over him for evidence. She was sure of a foreign odor. She put their relationship on a platonic basis immediately.

Their matrimonial canoe was now certainly over some rough waters. During the time of courtship, the young wife had thought Iktomi "cute," with all his faults and ineptness. Not so now. She was convinced he was nothing but a mouthy, cheating, lying coward. She said she wasn't jealous, but she took a sadistic pleasure in making him wince with those awful names she called him.

When the little woman's ranting got too warm, Iktomi went into a pouting slump. At times he'd climb the hill. There, with robe drawn over his bowed head, he sat the day out, presenting a forlorn picture indeed. The wife, too, was young and had much to learn. At times she'd have a bad case of remorse and would despise herself for berating and insulting Iktomi. As a way of making amends, she would then pretty herself up and fix tempting dishes for Iktomi and then coyly ask him to tell her more about the Fox Society, or the intricate aspects of ruling hordes of people.

Iktomi had considered the matter of "the instabilities of the female mind," and it was during such a time, when the marital atmosphere was more cheerful, that he took another long step in his scheming. In great detail he told about how the Fox Society had planned a prolonged war campaign. Only the bravest of men would be selected for the extended crusade. As always, the warriors were chosen by call, and he (Iktomi) was among the first to be led to the center, he said. He told how, in his acceptance speech, he had said in essence: "I am greatly honored. You have made a wise choice. I am the man to strike the enemy first. But I must decline the honor you bestow on me because I am a man who abides by the rules of proper conduct and to me, your provision regarding mothers-in-law is morally wrong."

The wife was a bit confused. What does it all mean? Is he really a coward for refusing to go? Anyway, she was proud that Iktomi was a speech maker.

Iktomi realized that his wife had missed the main issue entirely, so with patience and using plain words he told her that: "Warriors chosen to go on the extended war must be accompanied by their mothers-in-law; they will be the pack carriers." The wife sat speechless. Never before had she heard of such a thing!

This was indeed a long step. He must now allow a little time for orientation. In time, his wife would convey the message to her mother. He dared not speculate what the reaction would be. He knew it would take some time for the women to settle the problem. In the meantime, he spent more time in civic affairs, counciling, and other things to avoid the silence and the gloom in the little lodge.

The wife, filled with unclear thoughts, wrestled with Iktomi's statement. When she couldn't bear it any longer, she blurted out to her mother the sinister war plans of the Fox Society.

There now occurred another chain of bad days, much gloom and no talk. And then one day, just as the daughter had feared, her mother decided to accompany her son-in-law on the war trail, commenting briefly that the Fox Society was a helpful society, always first in war and "if that is their wish, it shall be that way." The distraught wife conveyed the message to Iktomi. He received the news well, outwardly, that is. What had seemed a hopeless dream might yet become a reality, he thought.

To allay any suspicion, Iktomi bitterly denounced the Fox Society for thinking up such a fiendish scheme. Taking mothers-in-law on war parties is immoral and against all time-honored customs of good conduct, he said with force and apparent conviction. He swore he wouldn't go. He would not be a party to such malicious scheming! In the same breath, he stressed the importance of the Fox Society as a worthy brotherhood; an asset in any community. He was fortunate to be an active member of such an exclusive society. Iktomi was never at a loss for words, but the important thing now was to keep the women busy so they wouldn't have time to think.

At Iktomi's urging, the women went to work making extra moccasins and preparing concentrated food for the long road ahead. Iktomi made much ado about sharpening and polishing a few rusty weapons. He was a little hard on the womenfolk, but he wanted to get the phony expedition off and away before some nosy busybody started asking questions. He prodded the women along mercilessly. When everything seemed to be in order, he hurried away, saying he would return with the latest war bulletin from the Fox Society.

Just before dark he returned, all out of breath as though he'd been doing some hard running. "We must pack at once. Some of the other warriors are already on their way. We must hurry and join them before they get too far away." Seeing the disbelief in the faces of the women, he hesitated momentarily, but soon was in control of himself and, if belatedly, he told the women that the Fox Society had admitted that taking mothers-in-law on warpaths was irregular. Therefore, the advice was that each warrior with a mother-in-law leave separately under cover of darkness. All were to get together later, at a designated rendezvous.

In the growing darkness, weapons, bundles of food, and extra clothing were hurriedly thrown together. At full darkness Iktomi took a tearful leave of his young wife, and stealthily, as the Society had advised, Iktomi and his mother-in-law marched away to do battle in far off lands.

After marching for some distance, Iktomi ran ahead and called out: "Where are you?" Then, covering his face with his robe he made a muffled reply: "Over here!" The trick sounded so realistic he repeated it often to keep up the appearance that nothing was irregular. There was no need for the tomfoolery; the mother-in-law had implicit faith in her son-in-law. She never doubted that soon they would join the others and then she would have other mothers-in-law for company.

As the night wore on Iktomi made more fake efforts to locate the other warriors. Always, the only response was the muffled reply: "Over here!"

Finally, Iktomi thought it was time to stop all the foolishness and make camp for the night. He soon erected a neat little grass hut. Up to now they had maintained the strictest of formalities. So, cleverly, he let his mother-in-law know that the grass hut was for her. He would remain outside and guard the premises.

Plodding over unfamiliar ground in the darkness was exhausting, so the woman made her bed immediately in the little hut, hoping to get a little rest without fear, since the son-in-law would be standing guard.

The night was balmy and pleasantly cool, so without effort the woman drifted away into slumber. Alas, a restful night was not to be. Suddenly she was awakened by an awful racket. It sounded like a hound dog whimpering in the cold. With the whining there was a loud chattering of teeth that sounded ghostly. It was Iktomi having freezing spells. "Hunhe" (Oh my), what shall I do?," he chattered. Deeply compassionate, the woman said: "Tima hiyu, okanye," (come inside, there is room).

Iktomi was inside in a moment. Nervously he fumbled around in the darkness, trying to get settled. Little gains add up to great victories, he mused to himself. The woman, being worn out, was about to re-enter dreamland when again, Iktomi went into convulsions with another freezing spell. Again the chattering teeth, the awful groans, as he doubled up in jerky spasms. Something must be done and done quickly, or surely Iktomi would never do battle against the enemy, the woman thought. "Lel hinyunka," (Lie down here), she said. Iktomi had never before heard sweeter words. Before a possible change of mind, Iktomi, eagerly and easily, slipped under the covers next to her warm body.

At last all his connivings began bearing fruit, the fulfillment of a dream, remote and seemingly impossible. In a warm bed, far from prying eyes, he now lay next to the woman of his ardent desires.

The freezing spells quickly passed away. With feverish hands he made preliminary explorations. His findings were most exhilarating. The natural smell of the healthy woman drove him to further probings. She, for the first time in many years, a male hand upon her, surprisingly felt a warmth that put her in a receptive mood. A male—so near; the darkness—so romantic! This night, after long years of abstinence, all the flame of her young girlhood gushed

112

forth at the fondling of Iktomi's eager hands. As the Lakota say: "Like a flower in bloom, a woman is fairest to look upon when in heat of passion." All scruples of impropriety gently and noiselessly tiptoed out of the little grass hut.

On the following day, remorse set in. There were no extenuating alibis as throes of guilt feelings gnawed at the mind. There was nothing to appease the claws of sin. Iktomi wandered off somewhere, perhaps to gloat over his conquest. The woman remained in the grass shack all day. At mealtime she passed food to Iktomi but she could not face him; she felt ashamed. Thus a day of self-recrimination followed a night when life's tenderest offerings held sway.

It was a long, long day, but as it waned, the pains of remorse had eased, and in the approaching darkness, the stars once again twinkled hopefully. She felt a pleasant sensation at the sound of Iktomi's footsteps. At the touch of his hand, the cruel mental pain faded away and, as they prepared to retire, those nagging feelings of guilt once again slipped away.

A long and idyllic honeymoon ensued, the kind of which many women dream. They had need of each other. He appreciated her experience and mature understanding. She needed him because, once again, she felt like a woman.

The beautiful southern hills were theirs to roam. Sometimes they camped high on the hilltops where the scented pine trees shaded and moaned over them. Deep down in the canyons, they bathed in the warm waters with only the moon watching and giving its approval. They had no schedule or timetable; they moved only when they wished!

Iktomi hunted and brought in the game, and she, an experienced woman, cured the meats and tanned the hides. In a little while they had a large tipi to live in, and their garments were of the softest hides. Because the woman was still young and fertile, the children came, sometimes in pairs. In a few years they had a sizable brood, a healthy growing family of which any good man would be justly proud. The woman was contented with her lot, to mother and fuss over her brood. Not so for Iktomi.

The marriage couch seemed a little lumpy now, and Iktomi grew irritable. He felt stymied in this life of exile. He had an image of himself as a man destined for big things. He wanted to be where people could recognize and appreciate his capabilities. The woman knew better. He would always be an ordinary man who, luckily, sired healthy children, an enviable status for many men.

His daily haranguing wore the woman down. One day, they took down their tipi and made their way homeward. Iktomi was jubilant, his dreams of being a public figure would be put to the test, he dreamed. The woman, being more sensible, knew there would be bad times ahead.

After many weary days of trekking and searching, they came at last upon the encampment of their own people. His ego unshakable, he was full of optimistic plans. He told his troubled woman not to worry. He had out-witted wisemen before. "Wait and see! When I tell those stern-faced, sleepy members of the Council, how I, single-handedly, kept the enemy at bay, the whole village will appreciate my valorous deeds and will re-instate us back in the good graces of its society."

Early in the morning, Iktomi and his family sat on a hilltop on the outskirts of the large encampment. A scout doing early sentry duty saw them, and gave them the welcome sign to enter the village. Eager to get things straightened out, Iktomi requested an immediate audience with the elders of the council.

Appearing before the council, he narrated a masterful tale. He blamed the Fox Society for tricking them into committing what seemed to be a serious social offense, but the elders must withhold their judgment. He and his mother-in-law had at all times maintained the strictest of moral decorum, he asserted. They were blameless of any misconduct.

The children? Oh—! Oh yes. Without the quiver of an eyelash, Iktomi told a gripping tale of heroism in which, he alone, fought off a band of *Toka* (enemy). He slew the enemy warriors, but a courageous warrior is also merciful; he never slays helpless children. Thus, he was obliged to bring the toka children back with him. The stern-faced elders sat motionless, unimpressed.

At a given signal, many braves formed a gauntlet and jerked off their breechclouts and as Iktomi and his woman came running through, each brave took a swat with their loinskins at the culprits. A punishment not painful, but contemptuous and humiliating. Only scoundrels and other rascals were given this treatment before being ostracized.

Iktomi and his woman were banished from the village. The children, always innocent victims in bad situations, were given away in adoption to families of high repute.

The moral? As the Lakota see it: "Do not live a lie. Do not defy social customs. Anyone's first concern must always be for the children."

THE SUN DANCE AND CHRISTIANITY

Edgar Red Cloud, descendant of the famed Chief Red Cloud, viewed certain parts of the Sun Dance as similar with some aspects of Christian ritual.

Red Cloud explained it this way:

"The crown our dancers wear is like the crown of thorns that Jesus Christ wore.

"The piercing of the chest once, reminds us that Christ was pierced once while on the cross."

The Sun Dance is vital to the spiritual beliefs of the Lakota. A sacred Sun Dance expresses the hopes, the longing, the prayers, and the needs of the Lakota.

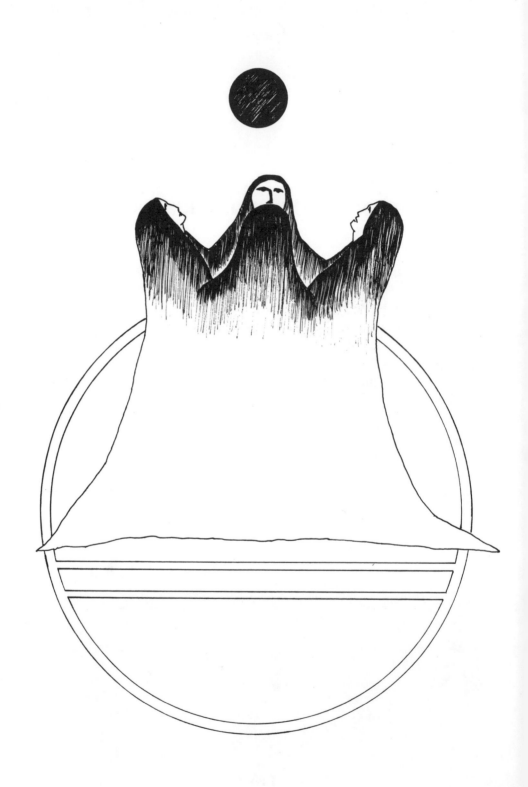

Tossing The Ball

Tossing up the ball (*Tapa Wanka Yeyapi*) a legend of old, is a harmonious blend of romance and mysticism, with deep, religious overtones. This rite has also been designated as one of the seven rites of the Lakota people.

Tossing up the ball was not a contest of skill in the true sense of competitive physical action, but rather a more sportive, social engagement in which the main instrument of play was a light, bouncy ball. The ball was made of tightly compressed buffalo hair covered over with buffalo hide. Within the ball, so legends say, are resting all the essence of the universe.

First of all, the ball symbolizes the earth. Contained within it is the spirit of Taku Wakan and all the elements of the earth, rain, wind, lightning, thunder, light, air and the four minor powers that control the winds and directions. Thus, in a true, religious sense, it was a holy ball comparable in sacredness to the pipe and the bladder bag.

The native peoples take much delight in romantic tales. It was so in ancient times. It is so today. These tales of love were generally of women, young, chaste, innocent and beautiful. In this legend the romantic tale is different; it is about a young man. This fine athletic young man had not only won trophies in games of physical prowess but also wore eagle tail feathers in his hair, a warrior brave. He was the idol in all social functions of the young. It was

117

hinted that many a virgin maid had fantasized being ravished by the handsome young man and also many married women secretly admitted to themselves they could be available if an affair came their way, hoping perchance they might produce a replica of the young man. His name was *Zintka Zila*, (Yellow Bird.)

Legend does not say how many wives he had but the story goes that he was involved in an unbelievable romance.

On a day a long time ago Zintka Zila went far afield hunting for a much-prized animal which he hoped to capture. The days were long; the sun was hot and his water bags were empty. In need of a cool, refreshing drink of water, he followed a narrow animal trail down a gentle incline toward a heavily wooded stream. As he was about to kneel down by the edge of the clear, cool water, he was confronted with a stunning apparition, a beautiful girl filling her water bags.

Strange, he thought, he was not aware of any encampment nearby; how could she be so far away from all humanity? A further surprise was that they spoke the same language. He saw that she was delicately beautiful. Beads of perspiration stood on her brow, her hair was neatly combed and braided with simple ornaments. A soft, fringed buckskin dress, denoting a fine background, draped her shapely figure.

Puzzled, yet concerned for her, he asked about her presence in such a strange place. She explained that her small family was moving to another part of the land. Were they helplessly entangled in some hidden net force? As they exchanged pleasantries they unconsciously edged closer and closer to each other and then, they found themselves in a tight embrace. Slowly they sank down on the soft, green turf. There was no need for preliminaries for these children of nature.

The day had waned. The setting sun draped the evening clouds in varied shades of red. Then it was dark. Crickets, frogs and night birds provided the symphony. Occasionally a shooting star glided across the heavens, disturbing for an instant the even darkness of the night. Predatory animals coming for water, sniffed at the lovers and without harming them, went their way. In the east, a large, reddish star heralded the advent of another day. The two lovers remained together. Finally, she told him she must now take him to her people.

They traveled for days. It was a journey resplendent, with all that is tender and beautiful, but a strange one too. She was ever the gracious, submissive woman but what was it he was doubting. Asleep, he now had disturbing dreams. He saw her not as a

118

lovely female companion but as a white buffalo cow hungrily crop-
ping the lush grasses. The dreams evaporated when once again she
was the attentive, lovely woman.

One day, as they reached the summit of a high hill over-
looking a lush valley, far away in the distance, they could see a large
encampment alive with activity.

"Wait here, I want to make certain they will welcome
you." With that, the young woman ran lightly down the hill toward
the encampment. Being exhausted, he soon lost consciousness in
deep slumber. As suddenly, he awoke refreshed. Far down the hill
the woman was waving a shawl, a sign of welcome.

Being young and not quite self-reliant in crowds, he
wanted so much to be with her but she did not wait. Instead she
soon disappeared among the crowds. However, he surmised the encampment must be in a good mood as there was much laughter and
shouting.

Upon his arrival, there was immediate silence. A man
approached, extending a hand saying that he was now an honored
guest of the village and that, in a little while he would witness a
joyous game always popular with the young people. At a glance he
noted that the players were divided into four groups. One group to
the north representing *Wazia*, and one group representing the east;
another the south, and still another the west.

A man came out of a holy tipi nearby. Taking a position
in the center of the four groups, he raised the sacred pipe to the
heavens. Holding it thus, he chanted a prayer to Taku Wakan, the
Holy Mystery of eternal youth. Upon this earth, the children of the
earth, all Your own creations, are now about to engage in a game in
Your honor, he chanted. We will be happy for we will feel your presence here which knows no bounds in space and time," he said. Continuing the sacred pipe ceremonial, he requested the presence of the
keepers of the four wind flows as each is represented in this contest of
skill. Then, producing a perfectly rounded object, he blessed it over
the smoke of the burning incense, intoning that this round thing, the
earth itself, will be the only thing used in the game, a symbol of the
wondrous system, the world, the moon, the stars and the existence of
live creatures upon the earth.

The holy man retired to the tipi. After a slight pause, a
score of beautiful maidens made their appearance. In songs of adoration and verbal rhetoric, each maid was complimented as she
paraded before the admiring throngs. In the end, by popular acclaim,
one was chosen to do the ball tossing.

Again in a ritual of purification, the holy man permitted

the young woman to touch the sacred pipe, and then upon the pretty maiden's head he laid his hands, a gesture of profound blessing. She must now, with agility and strength, toss the ball throughout the entire game.

"Hokahe," he said (forward to your destiny!) The young woman, beginning with the group representing Wazia, tossed the ball high in the air. Many hands reached for it but the ball fell to the ground. A mad scramble ensued. Out of the writhing mass of humanity, a young man emerged holding high the ball. There were resounding shouts from the spectators, war whoops from the men and screech owl calls from the women. The ball was thrown back to the tosser.

Next, she turned to the sunrise group, because the north people had lost their second chance by dropping the ball. Shouting a warning cry, she tossed the ball to the east group. This time a young man, leaping high, caught the ball in mid-air. A big achievement for his group, for now they would get another toss. Again there was general excitement. On the second toss too many eager hands spoiled the East's chances for a third toss. The ball fell to the ground, causing another mad scramble.

In this manner each group had its chance to catch or scramble for the ball. Then finally, there was a big free-for-all. All the groups came closer together and the ball was tossed straight up in the air. There was bedlam with screams of pain.

Each contestant fought for possession of the ball because when the game was over, the lucky ones who caught the ball or who came through the melee holding the ball, like foot-sore, war-weary braves returning from the warpath, were heroes.

Next in order was the *Cantkiya* (exaltation) ceremonial. Praises were heaped upon each winner and he was showered with gifts. Singers sang their praises while drums boomed low thunder rolls. The parents of the winners stepped forward. Through the public herald, there was more praise for those emerging victorious from a wild, rough game. Certain persons were called upon to come forward and receive gifts. The recipients ran forward with their *Haye Haye* (exclamation of thanks) and did the *Ite yuwinta* (placing the palms of the hands on each cheek and drawing the hands gently down to the chin) upon the hero in whose honor the gift was offered.

All this, Zintka Zila saw. A strange drama of changing scenes; a spectacle of spontaneous merriment with no hint of sadness.

Suddenly there was deathly silence. Instead of his love-mate he so longed to see, it was again the man who had spoken earlier. Now he said, "You have been chosen many moons ago to be the prophet of the White Buffalo Woman and some day you will be a renowned leader of your people as the originator of the *Tapa wanka yeyapi* (Tossing up the Ball.) Today you have been privileged to witness the game in its entirety. You, *Wicasa Akantu* (Upon-the-Earth-Man) are endowed with arms and can play the game in a much handier way. You will now return to your people and teach them the ritual of the ball tossing. Many hidden lessons will emerge if you will play it well and many times."

Reading the longing in his eyes, the man explained that the lovely maiden belonged in another form of life. "A fruitful life with her is not to be," he said, "for she is the sacred White Buffalo Woman. Cherish and always value the memories you have of her. It is the end. The White Buffalo Woman, in many ways in the past, has shown your people the red road of life and will continue to be with you always."

The man and his words seemed to fade away. As if shaken awake from a deep trance he found himself a solitary figure upon the vast prairie. Far away a herd of buffalo leaving a trail of dust was fast fading away. Far behind was a lone white buffalo cow.

All predictions of the strange buffalo man came true. Zintka Zila, a holy man of much wisdom and humility, lived a long, honored life as the originator of the Tossing up the Ball.

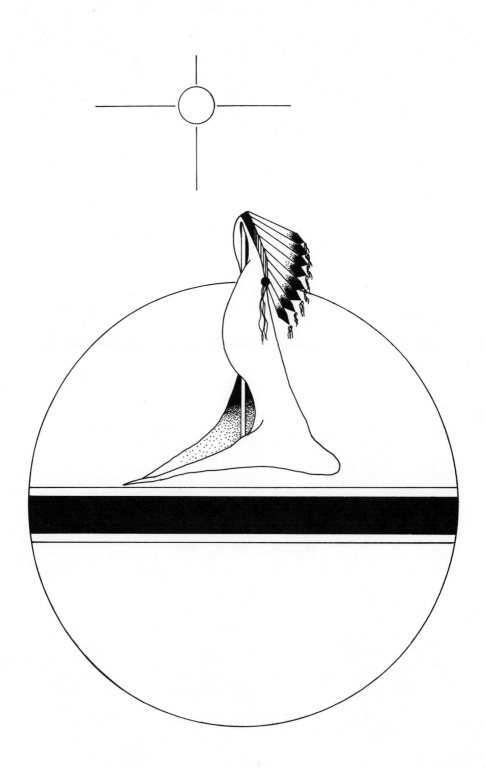

Ragi Gluha

THE RITUAL OF THE NAGI GLUHA, (retaining the soul) is a tribal ceremony. It was practiced up to recent times. Through the concerted efforts of the early missionaries, the United States Government banned this ritual, as well as the Sundance and other rites. These observances so sacred to the Lakota, were deemed to be barbarous, paganistic, to those who professed Christianity.

Origin of the Nagi Gluha ritual is not known. Some say it was the *Ptesan Winyan*, (White Buffalo Woman) who taught the ancient peoples to retain the souls of loved ones. The souls of men with exceptional minds were sometimes capable of being retained, it was said.

The Indian has always sought ways to draw aside the curtain that hides the mysteries of the beyond. "Keeping the soul" was one method by which much was learned, so they say, and the benefits gained served both the dead and the living. The art of caring and respect for your fellow beings and righteous living were lessons learned from the soul while in a transitional state. In turn, it was believed that the rituals of prayer cleansed the departing soul so that, when released, its journey toward the eternal land was pleasant and free.

It was further believed that a soul, kept in a tiny *Wopahta*, (a small bag) inside a tipi tied to the back pole made that tipi a hallowed place.

The Lakota believe that death is an essential part in the scheme of world order. Yet when death struck, there was much wailing and some acts of self-torture among those closely affected. If the grief was of unbearable intensity, the principals might express a wish to retain the soul. The next step was to dispatch a messenger to the keeper of the sacred pipe, bearing appropriate gifts. The keeper, a highly respected man, considered the request carefully. If he found the petitioners willing and able, he agreed to perform the rite. A herald would round up the encampment, announcing the ceremonial of Nagi Gluha. The people gathered, and singers appeared with their drums. They sang songs of encouragement, as the people wept.

The keeper of the sacred pipe, a man wise in the performance of the step-by-step sequences of rituals, took command of the procedure. In an opening chant he invoked the presence of Taku Wakan and the White Cow Woman, the presenter of the sacred pipe. Then, in short chants, he would act out all the proper stances of the pipe ritual. The ceremony was performed in the tipi where the corpse lay in shrouds. The sides of the tipi were raised high so the viewers could watch every movement.

The last and most important act was the taking of a lock of hair from the corpse. The lock of hair was then held over a pot of aromatic grasses and herbs which were slowly burning while the keeper asked the blessings of Taku Wakan and the White Cow Woman.

When thoroughly blessed, the lock of hair was then wrapped in a small buckskin bag and presented to the parents or to close relatives, always with the admonition that they were now assuming a grave responsibility, a duty answerable only to Taku Wakan.

When the ceremonials were over, and with a final burst of sorrow, the corpse was prepared for its final journey. A pinch of food or some personal belonging was included in his shrouds. Then the corpse was carried away and placed upon a scaffold already erected, or to some large tree, there to be consumed by the elements, the remains then to return to earth.

At functions of this kind, many useful articles were given away to the aides and performers. Other articles were placed on the ground for the needy to help themselves. Not required in the ceremonies, but always a noticeable aspect, was the *Lila Wicaceya*, (loud, mass weeping).

Finally there came the time when the soul was to be liberated, a ritual even more involved.

124

There was no exact time given for "keeping a soul." The time element depended very much on the emotional status of the parents or relatives. If they felt fully recovered from their sorrow and had accepted death as an unavoidable part of life, then the soul must be liberated. Also, the captive soul might want to be released and be on its way. (Grandmother said that if a soul was held too long, it became unruly and played mean, practical jokes on the living) There were other factors making a necessity to free a soul. The tipi where a soul was kept became a public place. The people living there had no chance for domestic life. There was no privacy.

In liberating a soul, the ceremonial procedure, they say, was much the same as when the soul was first retained, except that now extra hunting parties went out to bring in a certain portion of the buffalo which was considered sacred and must be used in the ceremonies. Also, there was the added ritual of selecting four virgins who must play important roles in the procedure. This was a special event in itself. Many innocent maidens entered the contest, brought forward by their parents or by sponsors. Each maid's virtues and womanly qualities were extolled in song and chants. From this group, the wise judges selected four to serve throughout the ceremony as maids-of-honor.

There was now a large accumulation of the sacred meat. This was prepared according to various special recipes. After blessing of the food, the young seated virgins, partook of the food. Then a wise and honored sage expressed the formulas for proper living: "You must endeavor to lead wholesome lives. Many bold young men with persuasive tongues will whisper convincing talk in your ear. They will hold you. You will be tempted. Restrain yourself; do not answer the call of nature. You will know when your man comes along. There will be pleasurable times for you. Teach your children to walk upon the red road (equivalent to the white man's straight and narrow path). Teach them to be mindful of the weak and the needy. Teach them to share their fortunes with others. Base emotions are harmful and must be repressed." Saying this, the wise man then withdrew.

The keeper of the sacred pipe now took command. In the center of the tipi, where the soul was kept, a holy stick was struck into the ground. A robe was draped over the stick; then a feathered bonnet hooded the draped pole. The makeshift dummy represented the body of the soul, which was about to be released. The four young maids took up various stations to act as receptionists for the many people who were now entering the tipi with gifts of food and other articles, all seeking personal penance or perhaps a final rapport with the soul on the verge of departing the world. Again, there was weeping and cutting of hair while the pipe keeper, calmly and with dignity continued with his chanting and gestures.

When the ritual gestures were completed, the keeper laid the holy pipe down, detached the holy bag from the pole, and went outside and faced *Itokaga*, (south). He chanted a special message to Taku Wakan to welcome the soul, which was now making a belated departure. He opened the bag and commanded the soul "Ho wana iyaya," (it is time to depart).

Since the soul had now departed, the ceremonial master retied the bag, with the lock of hair still within, and returned it to the parents or close relatives.

The ceremony completed, there was a sudden and complete reversal of mood. The wailing ceased. The virgins, now bright and cheerful, were feted and praised. The parents and relatives gave away valuable gifts in their honor. *Woyute,* (food) was plentiful; *Hayapi na Woyuha,* (clothing and other possessions) were piled here and there, ready to be distributed. The hungry sat in circles while the virgins rationed out the food and clothing. The children, by mutual feeling, gathered in groups and resumed their games with great sounds of shouting and laughter. The *Heyoka,* (clowns) went through their capers hoping to get a chuckle or two. The singers gathered round their drums bursting forth in rhythmic song, and there was dancing.

A SONG OF HEYOKA

Black Elk, the great Sioux, gave the following chant to John G. Neihardt, his biographer. First, he explained that in the Heyoka ceremony, everything is backwards. "It is planned that the people shall feel jolly and happy first, so that it may be easier for the power to come to them," he said.

Then this important observation was made, "The truth comes into the world with two faces. One is sad with suffering, and the other laughs. It is the same face, laughing or weeping. When people are already in despair, maybe the laughing face is better for them." (John G. Neihardt, *Black Elk Speaks.*)

> This I burn as an offering.
> Behold it.
> A sacred praise I am making.
> A sacred praise I am making.
> My nation, behold it in kindness.
> The day of the sun has been my strength.
> The path of the moon shall be my robe.
> A sacred praise I am making.
> A sacred praise I am making.

Puberty Blessing Songs

ONE OF THE SEVEN RITES OF THE Lakota is the Puberty Blessing Songs (Isna Ti Alowan). This is a ceremonial practiced up to modern times.

The phrase *Isna Ti* means living alone or to be temporarily in isolation. The custom of isolating women in fertility was a common practice handed down from ancient times. But the sanctification rites, songs of blessing and praise, feasting and the give-away ritual, only happens when a young girl has her first menstrual flow. The rituals were not for every young woman, but only for girls of certain families.

It was the general belief in those ancient times that men of medicine and magic were highly allergic to women in fertility. They say such women had a contaminating effect upon their artistry, so much so, that medicine men refused to treat the sick saying the potency of their preparations were rendered ineffective when such a woman was present. Or, in special sessions, men of magic could not perform their supernatural wizardry because their invisible helpers or the "little rock boys," so highly sensitive, were reduced to immobility and could not perform. Thus, to assure the medicine man an absence of pollution, women in fertility discreetly kept themselves in voluntary isolation.

The actual performance of *Isna Ti Alowan* as prophesied by the White Buffalo Woman, had all the aspects of legendry.

129

Oihanbleta, (Dreamland, or Vision-land) is a land of un-
reality, a sub-conscious realm from which, the Lakota say, much
wisdom has been gleaned. Sicknesses have been identified and cures
have been found. Discovery of edible foods, rules of behavior and
moral living, the awareness of Taku Wakan, were the end products of
men who dreamed, who dared to work out the essence of their dreams
to some practical usage.

So it was that a young man in the remote past had a
dream. In his visionary land he was alone. He wandered far and wide
over strange, unfamiliar country. Then one day, he came upon a
group of people intensely engaged in some strange behavior. So ab-
sorbed were they in their drama they did not heed the man as he
approached. When he came upon them, behold, a miraculous change
took place. The group of people so busily moving about were no
longer people but a herd of buffalo and the object of their intense
concentration was a new-born calf.

A large bull, bellowing and snorting, began digging out a
wallow with its fore-legs, now and then tearing out chunks of sod
with his shiny horns. Finishing the wallow, it came charging upon
the wobbly calf bellowing; and when he snorted, out came vapors of
blood from nostrils and mouth. The cow buffalo, seeming to take their
cue from the bull, got in line and advanced upon the calf, each taking
a lick until its hair was fluffy and dry.

The dreamer, perturbed over what he beheld, was startled when he was at last addressed by the large bull: "You are a
Wicasa Akantu (Earth man, a being apart from the spirit or animal
world) but you have been privileged to witness a sacred ritual. It is
our way to bless and cleanse the young so they may experience all the
stages of life, to give forth of themselves as mother earth spawns all
life in a continuing lineage."

Then, in the fashion of *Hunkapi,* (making of relatives)
the large bull, acting as a host, called another bull before the young
man. "This bull is to be your father." Again, presenting a more griz-
zled bull, the hosting bull said: "From now on this bull shall be your
grandfather." In the same order of ceremony, two cow buffalo were
called forward, one to be the mother, the other to be grandmother of
the young man. "In these four closest of relationships we now have
sealed a lasting friendship. What you have witnessed here must also
be the life-custom of your people. Return now and practice in some
manner what you have been taught here."

Once again he was quite alone. Far away, he saw a herd
of buffalo moving away over a hill.

For a time the young man accepted his dream casually

and was not disturbed. But as the moons of time passed by he became so obsessed with the strange dream that he felt impelled to seek the counsel of the village holy men. These men, wise in resolving and giving meaning to mental complexities, heard the young man's plea without much talk. After a time, they conceded that there was a message in the young man's dream. The perplexing question was: how to put the message in practice. Man was not properly equipped to lick dry freshly born babes. Human beings do not have a long, rough tongue. Why not bless and purify the young mothers-to-be! Thus the songs of praise and blessing over young maidens experiencing their first flow came about.

The young man was duly accepted into the holy order as a man endowed with the proper mythical powers.

A day came when he had a chance to put his dream in practice. A messenger bearing gifts and a peace pipe came with a plea that a young maid was in the throes of her first menstruation, that it was the wish of the parents that he bless her. As was customary he accepted the lighted pipe and in silence, sat smoking. When finished, he requested that certain essential articles be gathered and taken to the tipi where the girl was in isolation. A buffalo skull, a knife, a bowl of cherry juice, aromatic herbs, grasses, sage for incense and tobacco. In the center of the tipi, the likeness of a buffalo wallow must be dug and the dirt piled in a sharp mound in front of the wallow. Strict privacy must be maintained, only parents and close relatives to be present.

When all was ready, the young medicine man entered the tipi, picked up the pipe and tobacco, stoked the pipe and lighted it and as a beginning in all ceremonials, he performed the sacred pipe ritual. Chanting all the while, he went through the various stances invoking Taku Wakan to bless and imbue the young maid with wisdom and guide her in her first emotional stress. Chanting, he summoned the presence of White Buffalo Woman and other lesser powers such as *Wazia* (North) who renovates mother earth with covers of purifying snow; *Wiyohinyanpata* (East) who pushes up the ball of fire for heat and light; *Wiyohpeyata* (West) who pulls the blinds so the earth may rest in slumber; *Itokaga* (South) keeper of our images. And lastly, special tributes were directed to mother earth.

Again, from the eternal fire, he set afire the mug of aromatic herbs. Over the burning incense he purified his hands and with much reverence laid his hands upon the head of the girl. Next, he picked up the buffalo skull, held it over his head in the image of a buffalo, he bellowed and snorted like an angry bull. Changing his mood he gently herded the young girl to the bowl where she sipped of the cherry juice. (The legend is that the young man was so realistic in his snorting act that witnesses saw the red dust or vapors of blood from the nostrils) Taking the buffalo skull from his head, he laid it upon the mound. Expertly, with the red and blue markers, he drew upon the white skull the symbols of all the Powers who took part in the rejoicing ritual.

This being done, now came the last act. A morsel of meat, first being sanctified over the burning incense or aromatic herbs, was placed in the mouth of the young girl with the warning that she was now fertile. "Mother earth receives the falling seeds; nurtures them so that new life may spring forth. As mother earth you are now so endowed. It is a sacred gift. Be not foolish but, always in an honorable way, exercise your sacred gift. The morsel of meat symbolizes an abundance of compassion. May you never turn away from the hungry; be ever helpful and if need be, take upon yourself and suckle the young babe who has no mother."

All through the ceremony singers who had been engaged for this special purpose, sang songs of praise, jubilation and blessing.

The sacred ritual being completed, the holy man, after being properly rewarded departed and as a way of relaxation, the bowl of cherry juice was passed around for everyone to taste. The public, ready for a festive time, merrily went into their feasting and dancing. There was food and piles of give-away material. Crowds remained until the last bit of food was eaten and the last item given away.

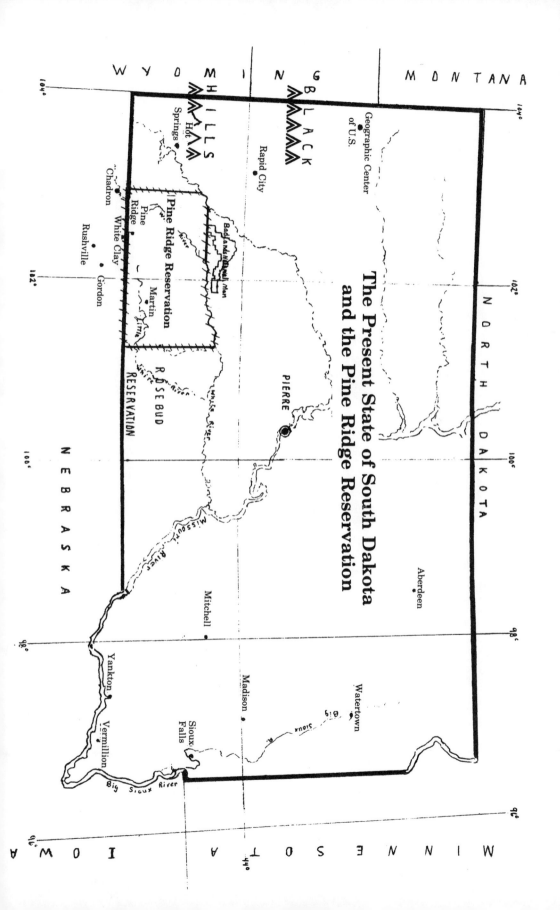

The Present State of South Dakota and the Pine Ridge Reservation

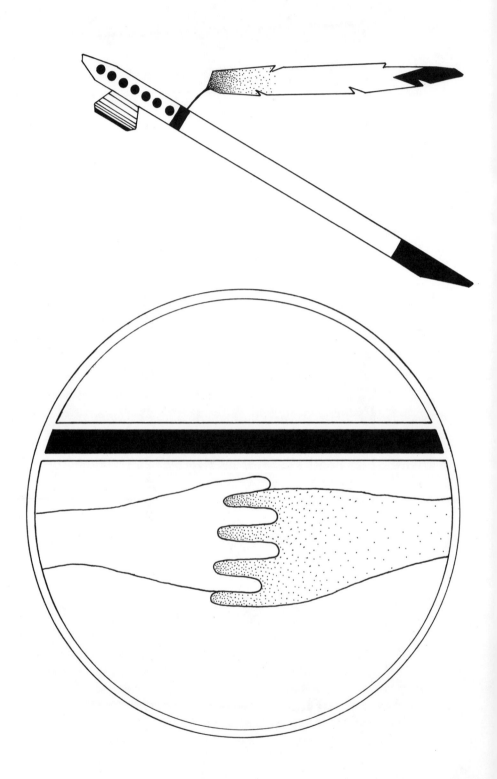

Ḥunkapi

ḤUNKAPI IS ONE OF THE SEVEN SACRED PRECEPTS of Taku Wakan for the Lakota people. Although the word is illusive with no traceable ancestry, it refers to a ritual in which, aside from marriage, two persons (or even warring nations) may, by mutual consent, enter into a new relationship. In cases involving two persons with no blood ties who wish to form a relationship, it becomes a ritual of adoption. The religious zest with which the rituals were performed made such relationships truly binding. When performed between warring nations the Hunkapi ritual was so extravagant, so say the legends, it took days to complete.

In a simple Hunkapi ceremony, a man may wish to become the father of a child or, a woman may wish to be the mother of a child, preferably a motherless child or, other combinations were possible. Such requests were examined and if found feasible, the ritual was performed. There were songs of blessing and adoration. The holy man chanted as he performed the sacred pipe ritual.

In ancient times Hunkapi was practiced extensively because, it is said, when the White Buffalo Woman first presented the sacred pipe to the Lakota people, inscribed on the red stone bowl of the pipe, were seven circles. Each was a precept of moral custom by which the Lakota must live. One of those circles represented the Hunkapi. (Those seven circles on the sacred pipe can be favorably

135

compared with the stone tablets of Mosaic Law. The Lakota lived a moral life by those rules.)

The White Buffalo Woman had ordained that the people must practice the Hunkapi so that they might be ever mindful of their Benefactor, Taku Wakan. His existence was an eternal truth. It is the will of Taku Wakan we practice coexistence and always extend a friendly hand, even to other nations. Those were imbedded in the messages chanted by the holy man as he performed his ritual.

The actual performance of the Hunkapi was not revealed by the White Buffalo Woman. It was only prophesied that in good time some young man would be endowed by Taku Wakan with the sacred powers.

Thus, in accordance with the prophecy, a young man, ever so long ago, was allowed the good fortune to preview the wondrous land of the Spirit World. As he wandered in this land of rapturous serenity, there was heard a Voice: "You are the seeker of the Hunkapi. Listen well, for it is a tedious ritual with many complex parts."

The young man, eager to join the austere society of the holy men, related his strange dreams in which he was endowed by Taku Wakan with special powers, who possesses the wisdom and knowledge to perform the Hunkapi in its entirety. He was accepted as a member.

Soon thereafter the young man had a chance to prove his ability as a holy man possessed of special powers.

In those days of long ago, the Lakota people were a strong nation. Other nations made war upon them but were never able to penetrate their wall of resistance. Then one day, a strange incident took place. From the lands of the cherished tobacco there came a party of *Toka* (enemy). They approached with signs of friendship. Hostile action was thus withheld, and the party was invited to enter the council lodge. They all bore gifts, especially long leaves of tobacco in twisted form. By sign language they revealed that their nation wished to make peace with the Lakota. The Lakota head men sat in silence. Only a young man of the Hunkapi vision, realizing the importance of the proposal, arose and addressed his people, saying that a lasting, profitable peace might be consummated if he would be permitted to perform the ritual of the Hunkapi. Shouts of approval arose from the gathering. Excitement grew.

The young man, by sign language, conveyed to the enemy party that the Hunkapi ceremonial must be performed, and preparations must be made.

To make the ritual of the Hunkapi binding in its sacred

mission of harmonious relationship, certain articles must be used and certain acts of procedure be religiously observed. The most important requisite is the sacred pipe and some tobacco. Other essential articles are the buffalo skull, sticks for a rack, pieces of dried meat, colored markers, eagle plumes, a knife, aromatic grasses and herbs for incense burning and the bladder.

Certain articles must be exchanged in the treaty making. These could include foods, war equipment, domestic animals, robes and clothing.

Before going further, perhaps, for better understanding, an explanation should be made why the lowly animal bladder has always been held as a semi-sacred article of necessity.

In every kill of the buffalo, many parts of the carcass may be discarded but never the bladder. After it is dried and the outside excess covering is peeled off, it becomes a soft, light, pliable, plastic-like bag of many uses. Many men of medicine use it as a container for their curative roots. The men of magic use it as a holy bag for their tricks. In various ceremonials, the bladder is used as the home of the controllers of the four directions. It is commonly used as a water bag. Sometimes it serves as a nursing bag for babies and cooking women use it as a mitten in mixing concentrated foods. When quilled and beaded, it becomes a handy trinket bag or as a container for valuables.

Continuing now with the ceremonial, the enemy party was instructed to choose one man to represent the party, preferably one with a strong voice because he must sing songs in the course of the ceremony. A holy tipi would be erected in which the Hunkapi man, representing the Lakota people, would make further preparations to receive the one-man envoy. With the big knife, he must clear a place in the center of the tipi. From the live coals of the perpetual fire he burns incense. Over the smoke he must cleanse himself and the sacred pipe. When all is in readiness, a banner would be waved and the enemy envoy must now come singing songs of lyrics heralding the significance of the new friendship and the alliance which was about to be made.

(Legend says that in this instance of treaty making, the articles of exchange were the corn and the southern long-leaf tobacco. Both items are considered highly prized commodities. The Lakota needed the tobacco in their ceremonials. The corn was a basic commodity for all nations of the Americas. During the exchange ceremonial eagle plumes were loosed in the air to float hither and yon symbolizing the pollen of life which impregnates all fruits and vegetation.)

The enemy representative now enters the holy tipi singing, and bearing his gifts. The Hunkapi man, with the sacred pipe and the ceremonial bladder already blessed, begins his sacred ritual. In a continual chant he invokes the presence of Taku Wakan to witness and approve the solemn pact about to be made. Then, in sequence, he summons the controllers of the four cardinal points of the earth. *Wazia* (North) who shields the fallen seeds with nourishing blankets of snow. *Wiyohinyanpata* (East) keeper of the ball of fire that gives warmth and light. *Wiyohpeyata* (West) who holds back the flood waters and pulls down the fireball so the world may rest in slumber. *Itokaga* (South) the direction we face to find our image. (Lakota legends say this is the direction we must go to walk upon the Trail of the Spirits, the Milky Way.) Lastly, the Hunkapi man appeals to mother earth to be present to witness the profound occasion of a new relationship with a former enemy.

Each time the Hunkapi man calls upon a minor power he breaks off a pinch of tobacco and puts it in the holy bladder bag as a symbol of that power. Then, with the red and blue markers, he honors each power by drawing their symbols upon the buffalo skull.

At the completion of this portion of the ceremonial, the bladder bag is now the home of all the minor powers of the universe, a bag now as divine as the sacred pipe. Thus, with humility and devotion, the bag is tied with buckskin thongs. After placing the lips to the opening of the bag, the Hunkapi man presents the bag to the enemy envoy with the admonition that he now holds in his hand a divine bag holding the witnesses to their sacred pact. Henceforth, they are no longer enemies but close relatives, in spirit, as individuals, and as two nations who must now live in peaceful existence.

Now the main actors come out of the holy tipi. Once again the pipe ritual is performed before the public. As a demonstration of good will, the head men on each side are honored with a draw on the sacred pipe. The bladder bag, now as sacred as the pipe, is also passed around so onlookers may touch it or hold it while offering a silent prayer.

Legends say those peace making ceremonies sometimes lasted three or four days, because each side must, as an act of good faith, divulge their war stratagems. Thus, all in fun, there were miniature war games. Sneak and surprise attacks, stalking the enemy and early dawn charges were shown. Then, in full war gear, there were charges and counter charges in which furious battles were simulated each side claiming more enemy strikes. After each session there were shouts and songs of triumph and exchanging of gifts.

As an act symbolizing generosity of heart, the dried meat which had already been sanctified, was cut up in small pieces. In keeping with the chant of the holy man, the pieces of meat were placed in the mouths of the enemy. The enemy, in turn, returned the gestures of generosity.

The Black Hills In Lakota History

BEFORE CONTACT WITH THE WHITE EUROPEANS, the Lakota had held the Black Hills in their possession for untold centuries. As the history is told by the elders, related over and over again to this very day, here is what happened:

One day a stranger appeared among the people. A man, covered with much hair, came to them, as the elders describe him. This man was welcomed by the Lakota, as had been their custom from time immemorial. Soon others joined him, and the strangers were welcomed. These hairy men were a source of wonder to the young. The older people speculated whether they were akin to the "dogman," or monkey. The Indians, generous as always, took the hairy ones into their homes, treating them with traditional hospitality. Soon still more came. The Lakota fed them, and treated them with respect and kindness.

The white men, however, with trained eyes for material values, took a panoramic view of the Black Hills. As they gazed at the magnificent scene, they saw at once the potentials of fabulous wealth. For them there was no alternative. They must have the Black Hills at all costs.

The Lakota loved the Black Hills for reasons vastly different. They held the Hills as a shrine, a sanctuary for both beast and

141

man. It was a winter haven for the beasts of the land, a traditional place of procreation, under the protective shelter of the pines and the deep canyons, a place for worship, where the spiritual yearnings of bewildered mankind were calmed.

The white man was contemptuous of the Indian and his religion. Greed for material things was a special element of the white man's character which the Indian did not comprehend. Thus there occurred the encounter of white man and the Indian, wherein at first only friendship prevailed and mutual benefits were exchanged. Soon the friendship and amiability turned to bitterness and hate.

The modern history of the Black Hills, after the entry of the European white man, is not a pleasant chronicle. It is a record of deceit, cheating, treachery and expropriation of the Indians' property. It is a record of aggression against the Lakota until the Indian was beaten. Ironically, he was beaten not by the sword and the gun, but by the written word.

Modern history of the Black Hills, as known and well documented today, has been bloody as well as heroic. Today the Hills, with its relaxing atmosphere, its beauty a virtual fairyland, has become a national playground. Thousands of people from many places go there to see and enjoy the wonders of this unique spot. In certain ways, it must be admitted, the advent of western civilization and technology has enhanced the natural beauty of the Hills. There are towns both large and small throughout the whole area. Highways now criss-cross the Hills. Gold in abundance and other valuable minerals are mined, and ponderosa pines stand darkly thick everywhere, and the sawmills are busy with the activities of the lumber industry. These activities contribute to the prosperity of the communities, (largely non-Indian) and provide the economic life-stream of the white citizens. Picturesque towns deep in the canyons, monuments, and other man-made creations have been born. I liked it best the way it was before all this hysterical activity.

The Teton Lakota were a strong-hearted, courageous people. Early in their history, they not only owned the coveted Black Hills, but they acquired and settled a vast territory. They held this territory tenaciously, involving a constant and vigilant watch along a perimeter thousands of miles in length. They had control over the prairies eastward to the Mississippi River. They held authority over the rolling hills westward to the Rocky Mountains and far into Canada in the north. The eastern slopes of the Rockies were theirs as far south as Cherry Creek, known as *Chunpa Wakpa* in Lakota, including the Platte Rivers to the east. This vast territory was theirs, up to the treaty-making era which began for them in 1851. (Eastern

Lakota people had made treaties with the United States before 1851, but these were merely admissions of United States sovereignty, pledges of "eternal" friendship, and for promoting trade.)

When the Tetons made their first treaty with the United States, they were recognized as owners of these lands, which were designated by the foreigners as "The Sioux Empire." This recognition of rightful ownership was the basis for all subsequent treaties.

The rise and fall of the Sioux Nation is a history all its own. Definite traces of Siouan influence can be found in the Carolinas. From there they migrated westward, leaving their racial footprints in the middle states, mainly in the Great Lakes region and in parts of Canada, where many landmarks still bear Siouan names.

The Lakota people were composed of many distinct bands. Some were villagers and planters who preferred living along rivers or near lakes. Then there were the bands aptly called the *Tiatunwa,* whose distinguished Native name was later shortened by the white man to *Teton*. The name implies "Looking for a Homesite." These famed hunters, in their ancient travels, discovered the Black Hills. From then on it was their "Promised Land," and from this focal point the Lakota expanded their vast land holdings. With the acquisition of land they flourished and grew strong, reaching their peak of stature and prominence by the year 1850.

Fateful events then shaped an unhappy course for the Lakota. Until this time they had always been able to hold back the encroachments of others. However, the white man, appearing now in great numbers, presented a new kind of challenge to the Indians. These white invaders and trespassers were not only shrewd and covetous, but they were ruthless. They seized choice lands and attempted to burn out the Lakota, who fought to protect life and property. Grasses and timber were set afire to chase away the game animals. This grim game of undeclared warfare between white man and red man lasted many years, years that were interspersed with discredited spurious treaties.

In early pioneer days there were many tragic incidents that were provoked by white men, so say the Lakota. Sacking and plundering of small settlements, stealing horses from wagon trains and from military posts were generally the work of white renegades. The Indian got the blame and was hunted down. The fiction writer also did his part in branding the red man as a vicious savage. He has been assigned a sordid and inaccurate place in history.

Despite this misrepresentation, the Indian has his own virtues. Innately courteous and honest, he is a true patriot. He loves his lands with a religious fervor, because he always has known he owes his life to the plants and the animals and they in turn owe their existence to mother earth, the sun, air, water and thunder. Thus, he worshipped Taku Wakan because He alone can plan these things to serve mankind.

This little book belongs to the Indian, and in it, without prejudice, his side of the story is presented herewith, as he struggled to preserve his dignity and guard his property against hopeless odds. This is only one part of a tragic story that ended in defeat. The march of relentless greed, as expressed in white civilization, overwhelmed and crushed him.

Starting with the year 1850 and until 1877, the Lakota have designated the era as one of treaty making. The Act of 1877 was never accepted as an agreement by the Lakota.

It was a disastrous era for the Sioux. In this short time of twenty-seven years, the Lakota, a proud and solidly unified nation, met ignoble defeat at the negotiating tables. Their mighty domain was cut to pieces by an arrogant foe who wrote solemn words of promise, only to forget or remember as the occasion seemed expedient. The Lakota naively regarded the white man's treaty words as something sacred. In two fateful treaties, the Sioux were dispossessed, parcel by parcel, of their own vast lands. Guile, deception and fraud were the popular weapons.

The white man, in his intrusions into Lakota Territory, was ruthless and destructive. There was wanton destruction of buffalo. The prairie lands were set afire, causing the starvation of animals and the destruction of timber lands. Was there a sinister purpose in this seeming madness? Was this a scheme to choke off the lifeblood of the Indian? The Lakota people had no choice but to fight back, and according to their factual tales and the records of the white man as well, they held their own against the invading hordes for all those years.

The United States, in the midst of this monstrous taking of Indian land and the wholesale destruction of the Indian economy, then initiated its first big treaty with the Teton Sioux. Using military facilities, large quantities of goods and commodities were carted to a region known as the Laramie Plains in Dakota Territory, where a mass meeting was held between the Lakota and representatives of the United States, September 1, 1851. The Lakota remember this meeting as the *Wakpamnipi Tanka,* the "Big Distribution."

In this first treaty, wide trailways were given up by the Sioux people for the privilege of unmolested white migration. They ceded other strategic areas for the purpose of establishing military posts by the United States. The military was to keep order in these new developing areas, in return for the concessions of land. The United States agreed upon an annual payment to the Sioux of $50,000 for a period of fifty years. Eloquent sentiments of good faith were exchanged, expressing the most solemn pledges to uphold and honor the provisions of the treaty. Goods and commodities were distributed throughout the encampment to bind the solemn agreements of the historic meeting.

Upon the return of the negotiating Commission to Washington, D.C., the United States Senate, without qualms, immediately trimmed the fifty-year clause as agreed upon in the field, to ten years, without the knowledge or consent of the Lakota. Thus did the Lakota have their first taste of official United States trickery which was to be the regular pattern thereafter. The Lakota, unaware of the Senate's action, trustingly allowed the trailways to be opened, and the army posts to be built, according to the treaty agreement. Later, the Indians were attacked from these very fortifications, which were originally intended to preserve peace and order on their behalf.

Now that right of way lanes were thrown open for unhindered travel, emigrants in large numbers moved westward in an endless stream. There was no end to the flow of white invaders, it seemed, fanning out in all directions. A wise observer in those fateful days, watching the mass migration, made this prophetic comment: "From where the sun rises the white man is coming like the flow of flood waters. Relatives all, beware! Hold your minds on alert, crafty white men are many." The sage knew only too well that his native and gullible tribespeople were no match for the wily white man. Many years later, Chief Red Cloud, in a pensive mood, expressed a similar view. He admonished the younger people, saying: "My young kinfolk, practice the art of lying; the day is not far away when you will be forced to live with the white man."

The Indian has always been depicted as a cunning savage practicing his nefarious schemes upon the hapless white man. The red man, on his part, was forced to form a low-grade opinion of the white man. He named him *Washi chu,* a name connoting a glib tongue, dishonesty and mercenary habits. Cheating the Indian was a general practice, and is so up to present times. Sometimes the Indian rebelled and reclaimed his side of the unfair bargain. Then he was called "Indian Giver."

As the pioneers moved westward in greater numbers, they ignored treaty agreements, aggressively and illegally entering upon Indian lands. Once again, there was open hostility. There was plundering and attacks of retaliation. The Lakota pleaded for protection, basing his complaints on the treaty agreements. He was ignored by the government and the military as well. He respected his treaty agreements and he was puzzled. Had he been tricked? Reluctantly, he realized that if life and property were to be protected, it was up to him to fight both the army and the restless, moving hordes. An eye for an eye was the rule of action. Retaliatory battles were vengeful and bitter.

Once again the prairie lands smelled of the blood and carcasses of buffalo and human. In the halls of the capitol building there was talk of doing away with the Lakota. Extermination by germ warfare or submission by starvation were some of the grim tools mentioned in the sacred halls of the nation's capitol. The slaughter of buffalo was intensified. The prairies were dotted with dead buffalo rotting in the sun. Smallpox flared up among the Lakota, spreading like a leaping prairie fire. Villages were abandoned, leaving the sick inside the tipis to die alone and in agony. They knew no way to combat the dreaded white man's disease except to flee from the victims. The whole western plains became a death trap, and the panic-stricken Indians sought refuge in flight.

For a time the Lakota, confused, disorganized, and at a loss for proper action, held mass rituals in which they offered sacrifices to Taku Wakan, beseeching Him to cleanse them of the devastating plague; to make them strong enough to withstand the diseases of the white man.

During those crucial times General William S. Harney committed an unpardonable sin upon a settlement of Lakota along the Platte River in the flat river country, later known as Nebraska. Harney invited Little Thunder, chief of the settlement, and his braves, for a friendly talk. While the general engaged the Indians in this fake parley, his army, numbering one thousand men, attacked the Indian village, killing women and children. A "savage" chieftain would not have stooped to such a dastardly trick. *Tiapa Wichakte* is the Lakota term for this type of viciousness. It means killing defenseless women and children in their lodges.

Along with the smallpox epidemics, misfortune in various other forms was experienced everywhere. The army, their would-be protectors by sworn treaty, was making open war upon the Lakota. The grassy plains were again set afire by white men to frighten away the game animals. Thousands of wild turkey perished in the fires. Crow Indians in the north country, allying themselves with the whites, made war on the Lakota, who had no choice but to defend themselves. Ammunition and guns still being plentiful, the Indian fought well, as history has shown, and for a time was successful in preserving his lands. He drove the Crow Indians back into the Rockies, once again controlling the Powder River country, choice hunting grounds in those early days.

There was open hostility everywhere in Lakota country, and the government dispatched emissaries to the critical areas to spread the word that the "White Father" wishes to make amends in a peace talk. Besides the gifts of woolen blankets, calico, sugar, coffee and flour, there were many glowing promises if the Lakota would consent to another treaty meeting.

By this time, there was much dissension among the many Lakota bands. The northern chieftains strongly opposed any further parleys; they had no faith in the white father's written word. The southern bands, already hopelessly integrated, had the stronger voice. Thus, in the course of a brief seventeen years, another treaty talk became a reality between the Lakota and the United States.

Once again a mass gathering was held on the Wyoming plains at Fort Laramie Dakota Territory. The Lakota named this treaty conference *Putinihin Sapa Wolakota,* the "Treaty of Black Beard." Officially it was known as the Peace Treaty of April 29, 1868, and was ratified by Congress on February 16, 1869. In this treaty the government established a permanent reservation for the Lakota. *A reserve upon which no white man was ever to enter,* or so they said. Since this reservation was to be of a permanent nature, the boundary lines were meticulously described, with the provision that all lands outside the permanent reservation, except as specified, were to be relinquished by the Sioux Nation. Thus, once again vast sections of the western plains became available for white settlement. For a brief time, after the 1868 treaty, there was peace in the Black Hills and on the western plains.

If the white man had honored his treaty bargains, history might have been vastly different. He had no respect for such commitments, however. Especially since the wealth-laden Black Hills were now within the confines of the permanent reservation, a potential powder keg.

Once again the white man poached upon Indian lands. The Lakota were not pleased and made complaints, but despite the feeble attempts by the military, more and more white men were coming in. But the Lakota, although severely provoked on many occasions, still had respect for the white father and those treaty words. The warriors were held in check.

In the year 1874, Custer, accompanied by a large contingent of soldiers, explored the Black Hills. In his report he confirmed the rumors that there was gold. When the news of the gold-find was made public, hordes of adventurers converged on the Black Hills, reducing the 1868 treaty to a mere scrap of paper.

That treaty of 1868 states in Article 2, in part: that the reservation was "set apart for the absolute and undisturbed use and occupation of the Indians herein named . . . The United States now solemnly agrees that no person except those herein designated and authorized to do so, and except such officers, agents and employees of the Government as may be authorized to enter upon Indian reservations in discharge of duties enjoined by law, shall ever be permitted to pass over, settle upon, or reside in the territory described in this article . . ." Those treaty words were considered solemn and sacred by the Lakota.

In this mad influx of adventurers, settlers, and miners on Lakota land, there were some legitimate prospectors, but the majority of them were riff-raff, the seamy element, gangsters, drifters, card sharks and greedy women, all looking for easy money. In the fall of 1874, and in the spring of 1875, in response to repeated complaints of the Lakota, the soldiers again made feeble efforts to move the white populace out of the Indian reserve, but since there were no vigorous demands, nor was any action taken, the poachers remained, in defiance of the treaty laws, and the orders of the United States were flagrantly ignored.

The Lakota reluctantly grew to understand that the white man's treaty words were not dependable. They accused the white father of keeping his eyes closed to the many wrongs perpetuated against them by marauding white gangs. There was no satisfactory response to the complaints. The Black Hills were now infested with white people; there was open hostility everywhere.

As time went on, the situation only became more chaotic. Open warfare might have broken out if some of the more powerful chieftains didn't have such a fetish faith in their treaty agreements with the United States government. Although the bringing of minds together was most difficult, there was a great deal of counseling. The northern chieftains, more belligerent, advocated a war to the death as the only honorable way to solve the situation. The majority had no desire for war; instead they petitioned the president of the United States for a just settlement regarding the Black Hills.

It is not known if the president heeded their pleas, or whether the United States sensed the gravity of the growing discontent and outright hostility on both sides. However, a Commission was sent westward for a grand parley with the Lakota. The written word has always been the best weapon of the white man, but in this instance there appeared to be an atmosphere of sincerity in the

148

Commission's desire to meet with the Lakota. The Commission was empowered to do some honest bargaining for the Black Hills. The details were made known beforehand. But, since the government preferred the southern regions of the reservation in which to hold its grand council, the northern chieftains regarded this with some misgivings. They felt slighted; already there was a gap in the unity of the Sioux Nation.

History describes this meeting as the "Grand Council of 1875." It was a gesture of goodwill, a little late in the day. Years earlier, or in an atmosphere of mutual trust, such a meeting might have been fruitful. At this stage, the Lakota were wary. In their hurt pride they held only mistrust and suspicion for the United States, its White Father, and the Congress.

After debating among themselves, the Lakota finally agreed to meet with the Commission. Powerful chieftains courted special favors, and later accused each other of engaging in underhanded dealings. With tempers barely under control, a site near the present city of Crawford, Nebraska, was agreed upon. The memorable council was held under a huge cottonwood tree on the banks of the White River, (whose Lakota name was *Maka izita,*) located a few miles north of Crow Butte, a historic landmark. To the westward was Fort Robinson, Nebraska, known as Red Cloud Agency at that time.

The purpose of the grand council was: To lease the Black Hills from the Sioux Nation for mining and other exploration enterprises. The Lakota named this meeting *Pe inkpa olotapi.* Its meaning is "to lease the top or the center of the Black Hills."

In opening the grand council, Mr. W. B. Allison, chairman of the Commission, said, "We have now to ask you if you are willing to give our people the right to mine in the Black Hills, as long as gold or other valuable metals are found, for a fair and just sum. If you are so willing, we will make a bargain with you for this right. When the gold or other valuable minerals are taken away, the country will again be yours to dispose of in any manner you wish."

Many were the regrets openly expressed after the close of that meeting. Some believed it might have been a wise decision had the Lakota accepted the Allison proposals in some form at that ill-fated but historic meeting. History might have followed a more peaceful course, with less bloodshed, it would appear. The original intent of the Allison Commission was purposeful and positive. This was no hoax. The men involved were eastern men, and they wanted to deal in a business-like way with the Lakota.

The many bands of the Lakota had now become irreparably divided. Certain factions wanted to lease. Others wanted to make

149

an outright sale. Still others had unfounded but strong suspicions that this could be another spurious deal. In any event, there was a grand display of oratory, including that classic phrase, "As long as the grasses grow and the waters flow." In the end, the Lakota failed to unite on any issue. The Allison Commission's proposals were rejected, and the grand council became dead-end history. The meeting proved one thing, however. Unity and loyalty among the Lakota were disintegrating.

After the failure of the Allison Commission, there were serious repercussions. Military forces, which kept a semblance of order and held full-scale fighting in check in the Black Hills, were withdrawn. This withdrawal meant that there was no law in the Black Hills, a virtual No-Man's Land. Open clashes, raids, and ambushes were common occurrences there and elsewhere.

The Lakota people, though accustomed to hardships, were now confronted with new perils. The diminishing buffalo herds were causing hunger. Rations guaranteed under treaty agreements were not forthcoming. Guns and ammunition, once traded and freely acquired, were now scarce on the market. Their economy had been systematically destroyed. On their meager resources, a sustained war campaign was now virtually impossible. There were other signs that disaster was imminent.

Solidarity and loyalty, once the backbone of the Lakota, was crumbling. A strange race of people was emerging upon the scene. This new hybrid race, slowly but surely, made its presence felt in all phases of the Lakota's social and political life. In their struggle for survival, this new breed, a part of their own being, proved a strong hindrance. The new race of people was the by-product of the many intermarriages of the white man into the Lakota families. These marriages were more prevalent among the southern bands of the Lakota.

The children of mixed blood grew up, branched out, and played a vital role in the thought processes of the Lakota. Their group personality exerted strong influences in the life-habits of the people, customs and traditions that had endured and even strengthened through the centuries. This was a force not to be denied in the fast changing events of those crucial times.

In thought, philosophy and life habits, the mixed bloods leaned toward their white progenitors. The former Lakota life did not appeal to them. They preferred to settle down and take root. They displayed acute awareness of their environment and saw clearly the inevitable fate in store for their Indian people. From their vantage point they saw a changing world and the inevitable, tragic consequences for Indian life. There were, of course, exceptions, but these were only exceptions.

This new and unique race, with a strong will of its own, was breaking away from the tribal womb, the traditions, beliefs, religious philosophy. Brothers, sisters and cousins, close relatives and faithful friends, all grouped in a clannish unit, were drifting away from a life which, they believed, would soon be outmoded. The Lakota Nation was disintegrating.

"Taming the West" is a slogan suggestive of bravery, toughness, implying heroic glory. It is an imaginary crown that many a westerner has hankered to wear. The crown has been generously passed around and placed upon the head of many a westerner, some deserving and some not so deserving. The Lakota had his own way of evaluating many of these characters; some of them did not fare too well in this evaluation.

During the critical times of the 1870's, the Oglala, under Chief Red Cloud, stood divided. The Rosebud Brules', under Chief Spotted Tail, stood divided. In the history books and in accounts of warfare, the name Red Cloud is legendary. There is a certain aura of romance and brilliance in the name. However, in the tragic years of their final defeat, Chief Red Cloud's contemporary chieftains branded him a collaborationist. This stigma overshadowed his early career as a fearless warrior and a skillful diplomat. Chief Spotted Tail was also given the uncomplimentary name of "switcher," which could be compared to the modern day fence-rider.

While the Lakota Nation was slowly falling apart, the chieftains of the northern bands were the true patriots. They vowed to carry the spear of war forward to the very end of the trail. Many warriors from the Brule and the Oglala forsook their kinship and joined forces with the northern Lakota. They felt the time was now, to give a life if need be, to make one last effort to retake the Black Hills, which was now in possession of the white man.

The United States was incensed over the Lakota's refusal to hand over the Black Hills. It was agreed that the Lakota had to be crushed.

While many bands of the northern Lakota, believing they were protected by treaty rights, were subsisting on game hunted in the Powder River country, momentous war plans were taking shape in Washington. A military expedition of great magnitude, a dream of the War Department, was quickly becoming a reality. The war lords, gaining the upper hand, had decided to invade Lakota country. "Crush the Sioux" was their war cry. General Sheridan was chosen to head the three-pronged campaign to hunt down and destroy

151

the Lakota.

Generals Crook, Gibbons and Terry were to be the field commanders. Crook was given his orders: to march from Fort Fetterman northward until he found the enemy. Gibbons was to move eastward from Fort Ellis, closing in on the enemy. Terry was to take a southwesterly course from Fort Abraham Lincoln, Dakota Territory. The objective: to trap the Lakota in a pocket and force him to fight, crush him and then to blame him for breaking his treaty obligations. The word "massacre" would have been better for such a well-planned campaign for "total victory" over the Sioux.

The first contact with the Lakota was made by General Crook, on the Rosebud River on the 17th day of June, 1876. This was about 40 miles east of the main camp on the Little Big Horn River. Crook, losing heavily, withdrew from the battle and from further fighting. Crazy Horse was the young chieftain commanding the victorious warriors in this first encounter. After the battle, Crazy Horse and his braves hurried back to the main encampment to sound the warning, that a great number of horse soldiers were coming. Be prepared to defend yourself, was their rallying cry.

Some writers say that Custer was the victim of an ambush. In a campaign of such magnitude, such a thing was highly improbable. Scouting work on both sides was intensive and thorough. The army engaged many a Crow Indian to do their scouting. Each side knew the whereabouts of the enemy, and a big clash was inevitable. Only the time and place were uncertain.

The fateful day fell on the 25th day of June, 1876. The military expedition of General Sheridan met its Waterloo near this little stream known as the Greasy Grass. Colonel Custer and his unit of the 7th Cavalry were annihilated. Major Reno's command was cut to pieces, the survivors taking refuge in the high hills westward. Crook's army, still licking its wounds somewhere, took no part in the final battles. But this last heroic stand of the Lakota—victors in the battle of the Little Big Horn—was a fruitless glory!

In history books and in paintings Custer is pictured as a martyr, dying in a blaze of glory, fighting off a horde of savages. However, despite all these accounts, the Lakota say Custer committed suicide. Their version is that, in the last stages of the battle, when dead horses and men lay strewn in disorder, Crazy Horse approached Custer with one arm raised high. Strangely enough, instead of shooting him down, Custer drew his hand gun and turned the weapon upon himself. The Indians further say that Crazy Horse had never wanted to harm Custer. He had in fact, instructed his warriors to take Custer alive if possible. Crazy Horse's plan was to take Custer captive and use him as a hostage. If the Lakota version of the Custer incident is true, why was it suppressed and kept out of the history books? A Nation's glorious record was at stake. The soldiers who fell there must have a hero's image. Crow scouts witnessed the suicide, so says the unrecorded story.

The number of braves supposedly swarming all over the hapless soldiers has always been grossly exaggerated. Fully three-fourths of the fighting strength of the Lakota were in the southlands within their reservation.

When the news of the disastrous Sheridan's campaign reached Washington and the public, there was bedlam. The whole nation went into frenzied, angry mourning. Delegations stormed the Capitol demanding immediate reprisals. They cursed the "red savages" for daring to fight back. They forgot it was the U.S. armies who went hunting for the Lakota with the avowed purpose to annihilate him. Irate groups demanded usurpation of the Black Hills despite treaty obligations.

After the battle of the Little Big Horn, and while the fighting forces of Crazy Horse and Sitting Bull were in Canada, the United States soldiers, in vengeful fury, went on a wild, marauding rampage, killing many innocent Indians and subjecting others to indescribable cruelties.

The era leading to the Battle of the Little Big Horn and some years after were the most difficult times for the Lakota. The buffalo, once their economic mainstay, had virtually disappeared. Rations and commodities guaranteed him in treaties, did not always reach him, or arrived so late that hunger stalked the people. The reasons for such delinquency on the part of the government were never explained. There was mass hunger.

In earlier times that segment of government known as Indian Affairs was freely used as a political dumping ground. The pay was small, but the possible fringe benefits held great promise. What shenanigans went on with government appropriations at that time has been questioned many times. The government officials have been accused of stealing Indian commodities, selling their assigned goods and rations, and generally making a nice profit at the cost of Indian hunger. One reservation agent has said he saw to it that the Indians got half and he got half.

To keep from starving, the Indians left their reservation and foraged for whatever food they could find. The angry soldiers hunted down these small bands and subjected them to atrocities no matter how innocent the Indians were of any wrongdoing. Their horses were herded together and shot down en masse. Young women were assaulted and ganged. Tipis were hacked down with axes. Weapons were gathered up and destroyed, and their worldly possessions were thrown in heaps and set afire. Then they were herded on foot to the nearest loading docks along the Missouri River, loaded onto cattle barges, and pushed out to float down the river. The barges had no facilities for human beings. One can imagine the suffering they must have endured. It is said that many children and the weaker members died enroute, the dead being disposed of in the water. Those who survived the trip were unloaded at Fort Thompson and other points along the river, where they were held prisoners. In these prison compounds many more died of malnutrition, dysentery and smallpox.

As an admission of guilt, at a later time, the Government permitted the survivors to make claims for all property destroyed in those raids by the military.

There was an old freight trail leading out of Chamberlain, South Dakota, winding its way in a southwesterly direction until it reached Oak Creek in Mellette County, South Dakota. This trail then turned westward and traversed both the original Rosebud and Pine Ridge reservations. The Lakota people designated this trail as the *Washigla cheya ukiya*. (Mourners weep as they trail homeward). It was called the Mourner's Trail because, as the survivors were herded westward, tears flowed for the dead kinfolk who were thrown overboard or were mysteriously whisked away at night.

At this stage, the Black Hills—Indian owned, was already infested with white people. Strong politicians, supporting the invasion, brought heavy pressure to bear upon the government, clamoring for an immediate takeover of the Black Hills, and the death of the treaty of 1868. The Lakota, too, had their sympathizers and there was a noticeable public reaction against the inhumane treatment of the Indians. Thus, when there was a story that a Commission was westward bound, sympathetic people thought relief was in sight for the oppressed Lakota. No! White Father had other plans.

This Commission, as it turned out, had but one purpose: to procure Indian signatures endorsing a document which, at that time, was known as the *Articles of Agreement*. This was a do-or-die assignment: to coerce the Lakota to sign away their title to the Black Hills. Mr. Newton Edmunds, at one time Governor of Dakota Territory, headed the Commission. He was an outspoken man, who had always advocated the usurpation of the Black Hills and the abrogation of the treaty of 1868 without any negotiation with the Lakota. No doubt, heading a Commission armed with orders to enforce his own views must have been most gratifying to him.

Before starting out, Mr. Edmunds requested that a contingent of soldiers be assigned to accompany him. He also requested that he be permitted to meet with the various bands separately. His wishes were granted.

The true contents of the *Articles of Agreement* provided that the Lakota must relinquish lands west of the 103rd Meridian. Also, they must give up lands in North Dakota, Montana, Wyoming and Nebraska, and consent to the abrogation of Article 16 in the treaty of 1868, which meant that the Lakota must also give up lands north of the Platte River and west of the Big Horn Mountains. In turn, the Government was to keep in force certain portions of the 1868 treaty. It has been alleged that the Articles of Agreement, as stated above, were never revealed at the various meetings, but only diluted versions were brought out for open discussion.

It has been told many times, that at those meetings, there was much confusion and tempers were barely held in check on both sides. Many believed (or were so informed) that the Edmunds Commission was a sequel to the Allison proposals of the year before—to lease the Black Hills. Much blame has been put upon the interpreters of the day—they were either very ignorant or were part of the hoax. The imaginary lines of meridian by degrees, which had to do with location of lands, were never clearly explained to the Lakota. Consequently, due to misunderstandings, there was much resistence.

As a result of the confusion, long after the enactment of the Act of 1877, though they lost the Black Hills and other valuable lands, many an old warrior entered upon the Trail of the Dead clinging to the belief that the Black Hills had been leased by the United States under a long-term agreement, thus insuring a decent life for his posterity.

As has been mentioned, this was a do-or-die mission, and the Commission resorted to every conceivable trick at their command. At all the meetings, soldiers with fixed bayonets were close by. Cannons were placed at strategic points ready for action. The Lakota were threatened with exile if they did not sign. The Commission members, taking note of the Indians' destitute conditions, also threatened to withhold rations and goods if they did not sign. Much whiskey was used to soften up the stiff resistance.

Bishop Hare, a pioneer missionary and a member of the Commission, resigned early in the expedition in horror and disgust. However, Bishop Henry B. Whipple of Minnesota was a strong spokesman for the Commission. The Lakota remember him as a harsh man who scolded them with scornful, insolent language, calling them fools for not "touching the marker," (the pen). There was much carousing and brawling, as some of the older Indians remember those hectic, so-called "friendly" meetings.

Despite the threats and the intimidating tactics so artfully used in the meetings, and the whiskey used to benumb prospective signers (indeed their best weapon), the Commission failed to garner the required number of signatures to make the Articles of Agreement a valid document. (Article 1, treaty of 1868, provided that if there is a further relinquishment of Indian lands, three-fourths of the adult males must consent by signature before such a deal can be regarded as a legal transaction)

After much time in the field the Commission returned to Washington with some 241 names. By their own count of the number of Indians visited, the Commission should have had 3,500 or more adult Indian signatures, which would have legally endorsed the Articles of Agreement. They fell far short of the required signatures. It has been alleged that names of affluent Indians were forged. At any rate, the Indians denied "touching the pen." Some Indians signed in a drunken state. Others signed because they wanted to be sure of food for their children.

The Lakota are protesting to this day. It is their contention that the Act was not a law based on mutual desire but rather a gun at the head act of extortion, a clear case of expropriation of property without recourse. Many have expressed the belief that usurpation of the Black Hills was in part a reprisal against the Lakota for daring to resist, and inflicting a humiliating defeat upon the United States armies at the Battle of the Little Big Horn.

The foregoing is a condensed saga of the Black Hills, a sordid era of deceit and wanton killings, and the final take-over. The white man has committed many wrongs against the Indian, but he doesn't lose any sleep over it because he feels that his acts of depredation are justifiable by right of conquest, or by right of might, whichever is more suitable. For the Lakota, it was a weary trail of tragic events culminating in total defeat. Now he finds himself confined within small compounds upon lands which, at that time, were considered worthless.

Today the Lakota is still on those little reserves withering away under the wings of a Government, once cruel and indifferent but now ignorant of their real needs and overly paternal.

Some years ago (June 2, 1924), (whether inspired by a guilty conscience or not, it is not known), the Indian was given citizenship of sorts, but he still remained a ward, many laws supposedly beneficial to him, have been passed, in most instances, without his knowledge or without his consent.

Today, the older Indians, elders of the tribe and nation, leave this earth resenting and distrusting a nation which professes close ties with a "real God," but disregards the teachings of that very same God. But the Indian as a symbol of freedom, endures as an example to the young of the country, a goal to strive for. The impact of his personality and way of life will always live on, identifying with all the ideals of freedom-loving peoples the world over.

To this day a universal feeling prevails among the Lakota people that the Black Hills belong to them, and will forever. A young warrior, Crazy Horse, expressed their sentiments when, in defeat and under derisive harassment, he so aptly put it, "Where my people fall and now lie buried, those lands are still mine."

The white man who came to Indian country kept his records, wrote about the Indians, the wars, ambushes and the final defeat of the Native Americans. More than anything else, the foreigners wanted the Black Hills. Like a precious gem, highly coveted, these Hills have been a bone of contention even to modern times. To possess the Black Hills meant wealth and inexhaustible resources to the white man. Some Lakota have sued for money in return for the Hills. Others don't want money. They want their Hills to be returned. Indeed the end is not yet, for the Black Hills are Indian country, Lakota country. In the end, these sacred places will be ours again.

Bear Butte (Mato Paha)

Approved by the National Register June 19, 1973

Bear Butte, one of the many sacred places in the Black Hills of South Dakota, was declared a national monument in 1973. The following explanatory statement was adopted on the occasion of this historic designation:

Bear Butte is significant in three distinct areas: geology, Indian spiritual tradition, and white settlement in the Black Hills. Geologically, Bear Butte is an excellent study example of a laccolithic structure because of its relatively small size and tectonically undisturbed surroundings. In comparison to other laccoliths, Bear Butte is young and possesses features usually eroded away on other structures.

From its discovery by the Verendrye Expedition in 1743 through the period of white settlement, Bear Butte remained a landmark for military expeditions, stage routes and wagon trails, as well as a place of strategic military importance. In fact, every expedition through the Black Hills makes mention of its towering, treeless presence.

Located on the northwest corner of the Hills area, the Butte could be seen for miles by prospectors, miners, and army scouts traveling toward the hills from Bismarck, the nearest rail head. Directly to the west of Bear Butte, Whitewood Creek emptied out of the valley leading to Deadwood and Lead, the most important mining towns in the Hills. Nearby trails and easy access to militarily sensitive areas in Wyoming and the Dakota reservations made Bear Butte an ideal location for stationing cavalry. Thus, Fort Meade was established near the Butte in 1878.

During the Sioux Wars of 1857 to 1876, Bear Butte was the site of many rendezvous, both white and Indian. One meeting of the Sioux Tribes near Mato Paha in 1857 is considered the largest Sioux council ever held.

Most significantly, Bear Butte plays a large part in the religions of several upper plains Indian Tribes. It is, for example, the central feature of the Cheyenne religion. It is both their Mount Sinai, on which the Great Spirit gave them their laws, and their Mecca, to which the Cheyenne prayed each day no matter how distant. The Butte is also a religious place in Siouxian and Mandan tradition. Religious ceremonies are still held on its summit.

Most of the Butte is owned by the state and serves as a

park. A good portion of the Butte's northern half, however, is privately owned and may now be in danger of commercial development. At least one group is considering urging the Game Fish and Parks Department to purchase and protect this important property.

NOTE: The usual historical inaccuracy is made in this description of the sacred Bear Butte. It was not "discovered" by the Verendrye Expedition. It had been discovered, occupied, and owned by the Indian people thousands of years before that expedition.

YESTERDAY AND TODAY

In modern times, the Lakota have shown leadership in the struggle of the Native Americans for their rights. Newspapers and television accounts have quoted their words as they insisted that the Lakota have certain inalienable rights, by sacred treaty with the United States of America.

"Today is a good day to die!" This was the call of the Lakota as they occupied the historic hamlet of Wounded Knee in South Dakota. But few remembered how this phrase originated, and who first said it.

Crazy Horse, Oglala Sioux, called to his men as he rode into battle at Rosebud on June 25, 1876, in a fight that saw the ignominious defeat of General George Armstrong Custer:

"Hoka hey! Follow me. Today is a good day to fight. Today is a good day to die!"

THE INDIAN HISTORIAN PRESS

An all-Indian publishing house founded by the American Indian Historical Society in 1969. Publishes at least ten books a year in history, culture, current affairs, and literature.

This unique publishing venture started in response to the inaccuracies and misrepresentations found in the commercial textbooks used in the schools.

Some of the books published:
Textbooks and the American Indian
Give or Take a Century, Joseph Senungetuk (An Eskimo Chronicle)
Tsali, a Cherokee hero, Denton Bedford
Indian Voices, Convocation of American Indian Scholars
The American Indian Readers in anthropology, history, literature, Education, Current Affairs (5 books)
When Navajos Had Too Many Sheet, George Boyce
The Right to be Indian, E. Schusky
The Only Land I Know, Adolph Dial, David Eliades
The Pueblo Indians, Joe S. Sando
Pima and Papago Ritual Oratory, Donald Bahr

Write for Catalog:
THE INDIAN HISTORIAN PRESS
1451 Masonic Ave.
San Francisco, Ca. 94117